THE MAKING OF INEQUALITY

To Caitlin

The Making of Inequality

Women, Power and Gender Ideology in the Irish Free State, 1922–1937

MARYANN GIALANELLA VALIULIS

FOUR COURTS PRESS

Set in 11.5 pt on 13.5 pt Ehrhardt MT for
FOUR COURTS PRESS LTD
7 Malpas Street, Dublin 8, Ireland
www.fourcourtspress.ie
and in North America for
FOUR COURTS PRESS
c/o IPG, 814 N Franklin St, Chicago, IL 60622

A catalogue record for this title is available
from the British Library.

ISBN 978-1-84682-792-1

Printed in England,
by TJ International, Padstow, Cornwall

Table of contents

Acknowledgments

This study has been so many years in coming to fruition that it is embarrassing, and the number of people I am indebted to constitute a long and distinguished list. I thank them all. For 18 years, I was privileged to be Director of the Centre for Gender and Women's Studies, Trinity College, Dublin, and I owe a huge debt of gratitude to my colleagues and my students. It was an honour to share your experiences.

I was also very fortunate to have Peter O'Connell as my agent. He worked his magic for me. Every book needs an editor and I was privileged to work with Sam Tranum and the team at Four Courts Press. I appreciated their kindness. I also want to thank Karen Vaughan for her creativity in designing the cover of this book. They were all terrific.

Certain people need to be acknowledged specifically: the late Professor Risteard Mulcahy who was always so very encouraging; my very special support group: Linda Doyle, Maureen Flanagan, Phil Kilroy, Margaret MacCurtain, Jane Ohlmeyer, and Deirdre Raftery; and above all my family who put up with me through the euphoria and doldrums of writing a book – to my son-in-law, Michael Hollas, my very special daughter, Caitlin; and my husband, Tony, who has always been my biggest fan and supporter. All of you were great! Thank you.

Abbreviations

BMH	Bureau of Military History, Dublin
DD	*Dáil Debates*
GAA	Gaelic Athletic Association
GPO	General Post Office, Dublin
ICA	Irish Citizen Army
INTO	Irish National Teachers' Organisation
IPP	Irish Parliamentary Party
IRA	Irish Republican Army
IRB	Irish Republican Brotherhood
IWWU	Irish Women Workers' Union
MA	Military Archives, Dublin
MDDC	Mary Immaculate Modest Dress and Deportment Crusade
MPC	Military Pensions Collection, Dublin
MS	manuscript
NA	National Archives, Dublin
NLI	National Library of Ireland
NUWGA	National University Women Graduates' Association
SPOD	State Paper Office, Dublin
SD	*Seanad Debates*
TUC	Trades Union Congress
UCD	University College Dublin
WS	witness statement

Introduction

This is a study of equality and the Irish Free State. Specifically, it analyses the ways in which inequality became embedded in that state. It provides an overview of the formative years of the Free State. It analyses major, individual acts of the legislation on gender equality as they co-existed and impinged on one another to the detriment of woman as free and unfettered citizen. While each was important in its own right, it is how they interacted with one another and created the state of inequality that reveals their true impact.

This book is about revolutionary women and how their position changed over the initial years of state-building. It begins with the events of the revolutionary era which brought the Free State into existence – the Easter Rising, the Anglo-Irish War, the Civil War – and poses the question: how did the Irish struggle for independence travel from the Proclamation of the Republic in 1916, with its promise of equality and citizenship, to the Irish Free State, which embedded inequality in the legislation that governed the land? What was the role of women and women's organizations in this journey from equality to inequality? How was women's citizenship conceptualized?

It is well known in the literature of women's studies that, in times of upheaval, women's opportunities expand while, with the return to normalcy, their opportunities contract. In specifically Irish terms, I ask: how did the revolution shift from the seemingly glorious Proclamation of 1916 to the dreary and hyper-Catholic constitution of 1937?

There are threads I would highlight to answer this question which run through the revolutionary experience: the radicalization of some activist women, which posed a threat to a conservative society; the persistence of patriarchy, which allowed many politically active but socially traditional men to attain power and privilege; the authority and dominance of the Roman Catholic church; and, of course, the vast destructive influence of the Civil War.

It was an uncomfortable road to travel, especially for activist women who seized the opportunities presented by the turmoil in Irish society to prove themselves as comrades and give substance to their claim for equality, only to see much of it disappear. Cosgrave and O'Higgins, followed by de Valera, laid the groundwork for inequality and began to modify the definition of the ideal Irish woman. Women were thwarted by successive governments that embedded inequality in the legislative soil and frustrated women's quest for equality. This study attempts to trace parts of that difficult journey.

What becomes apparent is that the radicalization of some women came about through the events of 1916–1922, preceded as it were by the opening up of Irish society through the cultural revival, the advancement in educational opportunities for women, the quest for suffrage, and, of course, the Great War. All these events linked together to offer the prospect of change for women. It was not, however, without its reaction, without its conservative rejoinder. The attainment by women of total and complete citizenship was delayed and thwarted. However, while Ireland in the 1940s and 1950s was indeed a conservative society for women, in some important ways, the seeds of radicalism of previous feminist activities, which were driven underground, developed into what was to become a vibrant and effective feminist movement in the late twentieth century and early twenty-first century.

The promise of equality, the perseverance of patriarchy

On Easter Monday, Patrick Pearse stood in front of the GPO and read the now iconic Proclamation of the Republic:

> [W]e hereby proclaim the Irish Republic as a sovereign independent state ... the Irish Republic is entitled to, and hereby claims, the allegiance of every Irishman and Irishwoman. The Republic guarantees religious and civil liberty, equal rights and equal opportunities of all its citizens, and declares its resolve to pursue the happiness and prosperity of the whole nation and of all it parts, cherishing all the children of the nation equally, ... Until our arms have brought the opportune moment for the establishment of a permanent National Government, representative of the whole people of Ireland and elected by the suffrages of all her men and women ...[1]

The Rising of 1916 was the opening act in this particular episode of Ireland's quest for independence that included not only the Rising but the Anglo-Irish War and the devastating Civil War. It all would culminate in the establishment of the Free State. Paradoxically, while 1916 was a military defeat, in terms of impact and consequences, it was an overwhelming success.

The Rising of 1916 expanded the players in the nationalist drama. For some women, 1916 gave them the opportunity to move into the public sphere 'to do their bit for Ireland', as the activist and author Margaret Skinnider stated, and take a dynamic role in the struggle for independence.[2] The Rising was the beginning of their participation in the dangerous and difficult war against the British. Women were there

---

1 Poblacht Na hÉireann, reproduced in Declan Kiberd & P.J. Mathews (eds), *Handbook of the Irish revival* (Dublin, 2015), pp 104–5. 2 Margaret Skinnider, *Doing my bit for Ireland* (New York, 1917).

when bullets were flying, buildings were burning and the surrender was ordered. Their participation violated traditional gender norms, but established a pattern for their subsequent activities in the armed struggle: they cooked, they performed first aid, they slipped through barricades to deliver messages. In effect, they performed a number of what were essentially private-sphere activities in the public sphere, and in so doing, I would argue, many of these women were radicalized.

Some women were armed and fought in uniform as soldiers. In an interesting application of martial discipline, when firing a gun, it was expected that the shooter would be in uniform. Margaret Skinnider had great fun with this, slipping in and out of uniform, depending on her activities.[3] Pearse mistakenly believed that if Irish soldiers were in uniform, they would be treated as prisoners of war if captured. They were not.

The Proclamation of 1916, however, did more than provide women with the opportunity to fight for independence. In many respects, the Proclamation was the showpiece of the Rising, the document that would undergird the revolution. It was often quoted and cited, especially by women. The ideology of 1916 as outlined in the Proclamation was one of equality and inclusion. As such, it was addressed to both men and women and spoke of 'equal rights and equal opportunities [for] all of its citizens'.[4]

Women's citizenship was a particularly important idea in the Proclamation. The 1916 document declared that women were citizens of the new state, complete with the right to participate in the public sphere. In the immediate circumstances of 1916, it meant that women were part of the nation-in-arms, those who would participate in staging the rebellion and go on to be part of the revolutionary struggle. This had a direct impact on the participants of the Rising. For example, when Commandant Michael Mallin said that he did not want women to go on a dangerous mission, Margaret Skinnider answered that:

> we had the same right to risk our lives as the men; that in the constitution of the Irish Republic, women were on an equality with men. For the first time in history, indeed a constitution had been written that incorporated the principle of equal suffrage.[5]

---

3 For a very interesting discussion of gender roles during the Rising, see Lisa Weihman, 'Doing my bit for Ireland: transgressing gender in the Easter Rising', *Éire-Ireland*, 39:3–4 (Fall/Winter, 2004), *passim*. 4 'Poblacht Na hÉireann' in Kiberd & Mathews, *Handbook of the Irish revival*, pp 104–5. 5 Skinnider, *Doing my bit for Ireland*, p. 143.

Skinnider's response was typical of a number of the women who participated in 1916. To cite another example, when the order to surrender came, some women insisted on surrendering with the men or staying in the GPO until everyone left. Louise Gavan Duffy remembers that:

> We were told to evacuate the building on Thursday evening, that all the women were to go out under a Red Cross flag. ... We went to Mr Pearse and said that we did not want to go, that we wanted to stay.[6]

In a similar vein, in their witness statements, Annie O'Brien and Lily Curran remember that: they abhorred the idea of surrender: 'We Cumann na mBan fell in behind the Volunteers. They [the Volunteers] had tried to persuade us to go home, but we refused, saying we would stick it out to the end.'[7] The women of Cumann na mBan took the Proclamation seriously and believed that they had a direct stake in the fight for independence.[8] It certainly conferred legitimacy on feminist aspirations. Their belief in the Proclamation and all it stood for would be an important factor in their upcoming participation in the Anglo-Irish War as well as their vocal denunciation of and rejection of the Treaty.

The Proclamation also spoke of universal suffrage – a well-known feminist demand. By promising equal rights and equal opportunities, as well as universal suffrage, it bridged the divide between nationalism and feminism. For those nationalist feminist women who wanted the vote but would not ask for it from a 'foreign Parliament', it solved their dilemma. As one group of nationalist, feminist women said in 1917: 'The Republican Proclamation granted equal rights to all citizens, men and women, and such being the case, there could be no talk of struggling for the vote. ... [T]he vote had been given to Irishwomen by Irishmen.'[9]

The Proclamation of the Republic vindicated the arduous work women had done for the national cause – be it in the Irish Citizen Army, Inghinidhe na hÉireann, the Gaelic League or Sinn Féin. It is true that men like James Connolly, Arthur Griffith and Patrick Pearse were open to women's participation – unlike John Redmond and James Dillon of the Irish Parliamentary Party. But what is more important is that women

6 BMH, WS 216, Louise Gavan Duffy, p. 8.   7 BMH, WS 805, Annie O'Brien and Lillie Curran, p. 9.   8 Ibid.   9 Minutes of women delegates, 19 Apr. 1917, minute books of Cumann na Teachtaire, Sheehy Skeffington Collection, MS 21,194, (47), NLI.

earned their inclusion in the Proclamation of 1916. As the historian Ruth
Taillon argues:

> It was not just because of Pearse's or MacDonagh's or James
> Connolly's progressive views on women that the Proclamation of
> the Republic included universal suffrage and equality for all Irish
> citizens. The Proclamation reflected the very real influence and
> involvement of women in the national and labour movements of
> the time.[10]

Indeed, women themselves were active and involved in pre-Rising
Dublin, especially in revolutionary organizations. Among these groups,
there was Inghinidhe na hÉireann, a radical women's organization
dedicated to militant separatism. Their dream was of a free Ireland
where men and women co-existed as equals, where women would not
be bound to a limited sphere of activity, where women would fully
participate in the political life of the state, where women would be
comrades.

The women of Inghinidhe na hÉireann were a vibrant, self-confident
group who challenged the status quo and joined together nationalism
and feminism. Their particular significance emerged from their ideology,
from their attitude. As the historian Margaret Ward has noted:

> Had Inghinidhe not existed, a whole generation of women would
> never have developed the self-confidence which enabled them to
> hold their own in organizations composed of both sexes. ... they
> rebelled against their exclusion and by their very existence opened
> up a whole world of new possibilities for women.[11]

Indeed it would be Inghinidhe's particular contribution that it challenged
the traditional definition of nationalist women by imagining a community in which feminism and nationalism neither conflicted nor competed,
but rather co-existed in harmony.[12]

---

10 Ruth Taillon, *The women of 1916* (Belfast, 1999), p. xvi. 11 Margaret Ward,
Unmanageable revolutionaries (Dingle, 1983), p. 86. 12 A number of my ideas in this
chapter are drawn from an article I wrote for an edited collection. See Maryann Valiulis,
'Free women in a free nation: nationalist feminist expectations for independence' in
Brian Farrell (ed.), *The creation of the Dáil* (Dublin, 1994), pp 75–90.

There were, of course, other organizations that had an impact on women and the nationalist movement: the suffrage movement, the theatre movement, the labour movement. As the historian Roy Foster points out:

> Though the relationship of suffragism to advanced nationalism is a tangled pattern, there is certainly evidence that the advocacy of rebelliousness, the desirability of imprisonment in a martyred cause, contempt for members of the Irish Parliamentary Party and the duty of assailing the representatives of British rule in public translated easily from suffrage to the cause of Ireland.[13]

Foster makes a valuable point about how 'the advocacy of rebelliousness' could translate from one mindset to another.

Through their participation in various associations, those who were attracted to rebellion became acquainted with one another and with the men who eventually formed the Volunteers and were particularly responsible for the Easter Rising. In general, there was a kind of fluidity to the atmosphere that allowed people to float among the various nationalist groups, exchanging ideas, debating differences. As Mary Colum, herself a participant of the period, remembered:

> Everybody I knew was working in one or several causes some people, working in all of them. Any public meeting by any organization for any movement would very likely be addressed by a selection of people prominent in all the other movements.[14]

In *Vivid faces*, Foster claims that there is a 'geography of rebellion'. He uses the example of radical Dublin to effectively prove his point. Living within a common geographical area, like radical Dublin, allowed men and women of compatible mindsets to come together and interact with one another,[15] to participate in suffrage societies, literary societies or even vegetarianism.[16] This was not just about seeing people with whom one had something in common, or going to the usual meetings. It was about developing trust, especially in the circumstances of 1916 and the

13 R.F. Foster, *Vivid faces: the revolutionary generation in Ireland, 1890–1923* (London, 2014), p. 175. 14 Mary Colum, *Life and the dream* (Dublin, 1966), pp 133–4. 15 Foster, *Vivid faces*, p. 8. 16 Ibid., p. 26.

subsequent guerrilla war. Witness statements are replete with accounts of young women looking for Volunteers whom they knew could vouch for them and establish their bona fides. For example, during the critical time of the surrender, de Valera refused to accept the authenticity of the surrender order from Elizabeth O'Farrell until such time as some of the Volunteers she knew vouched for her.[17]

One of the most important organizations to sway the minds and hearts of Irishmen and Irishwomen was the Gaelic League. Founded in 1893, it was committed to reviving all things Irish, from the language, to dress, to myths and sagas of a long-lost Irish past. Reviving the Irish language was seen as a necessity for the claim to be a separate and distinct nation, and in preserving Ireland's unique culture, conspicuously different from that of England. De-anglicization was a common theme throughout the revolutionary period.

More importantly, in terms of women's history, was the fact that 'it was the first organization to allow women membership on equal terms with men'.[18] In the early days of the League, there was an inherent egalitarian-ism – women and men were taught Irish in co-educational classes, went to Irish dances together and attended Irish summer schools. As they cycled off to league meetings and lectures, they experienced a level of freedom and independence that was previously unknown. Overall, the activities of the Gaelic League provided much more freedom than conventional society.

The Gaelic League, moreover, also provided cover for the meetings of various nationalist organizations. Madge Daly of Limerick recalled in her witness statement that:

> Soon after the formation of the Volunteers, a branch of Cumann na mBan was started in Limerick City. The first meeting was held in the Gaelic League Rooms, and the majority of those in attendance were members of the Gaelic League, or were girls belonging to families who had carried on the Fenian tradition.[19]

I would also argue that family was important in influencing a woman's desire to join Cumann na mBan and the Easter Rising. Perhaps the role

17 Ann Matthews, *Renegades: Irish republican women, 1900–1922* (Cork, 2010), p. 142. 18 Maria Luddy, 'Women and politics in Ireland, 1860–1918' in Angela Bourke et al. (eds), *Field Day anthology of Irish writing, v: Irish women's writings and traditions* (Cork, 2002). 19 BMW, WS 855, Madge Daly, p. 1.

of family was evident mostly in working-class families whose children were not involved in the 'generational rebellion' that Foster sees as happening in Dublin around the time of the Rising. Perhaps it is a question of class, with middle-class women becoming 'alienated not only from British rule, but from the values and ambitions of their parents and finally from the alternative offered by the constitutional IPP'.[20] That was certainly true of some families. However, in several witness statements, the women of Cumann na mBan point out that they came from a revolutionary lineage, saying their father was a Fenian or their mother was a nationalist. For example, Miss Moira Kennedy O'Byrne recorded in her witness statement: 'Of course, we were all brought up very Irish – that was the atmosphere at home, as my father despised everything English.'[21]

She remembers that when the Rising started, her father was very excited, and he went into town to see what was happening. He came back in a great state, saying: 'This is a fight for Ireland and there is no son of mine in it. It is the first time that none of our family is in such a fight.' In this statement, family meant sons and he explicitly joined patriarchy and patriotism. He was looking for his sons to fight for Ireland but instead he inspired his daughter. Her next sentence is 'After the Rising I joined Cumann na mBan.'[22]

In this revolutionary milieu, on the path to the Easter Rising, one of the most important new happenings for women was the formation of Cumann na mBan. Its creation gave women an official place in the advanced nationalist organizations of the country. Joining Cumann na mBan was a revolutionary act. For example, Brighid O'Mullane, an organizer for Cumann na mBan, points out that gun-women were neither acceptable nor respectable.[23] There was, of course, the Volunteers – but that was a male domain. There was also, the Irish Citizen Army, which accepted both men and women – and was one of the first organizations to admit and arm women as soldiers[24] – but it was also associated with the cause of labour.

However, it was Cumann na mBan that offered women a place in the contemporary nationalist movement. It was Cumann na mBan that was an organization of women-in-arms, women active in the public sphere – facts that defied convention. It was Cumann na mBan which, by its

20 Foster, *Vivid faces*, p. xxii.   **21** BMH, WS 1029, Moira Kennedy O'Byrne, pp 2–3.   **22** Ibid.   **23** BMH, WS 450, Brighid O'Mullane.   **24** BMH, WS 391, Helena Molony.

very existence, ruptured traditional gender norms. It is not at all clear who founded Cumann na mBan or what its initial purpose was. What we do know is that it was officially launched on 2 April at Wynn's Hotel in Dublin.[25]

Taken in conjunction with the promise of equality given in the Proclamation of the Republic – and the opportunities presented and availed of in 1916 and in the Anglo-Irish War – it helped to shatter (or at least suspend) traditional gender relations for the revolutionary period. The witness statements of some of the members of Cumann na mBan give testimony to the fact that women were taking risks, ignoring customary restraints, norms and conventions – at least for the duration of the revolution. Marie Perolz, who was active in Inghinidhe na hÉireann, Cumann na mBan and the Irish Citizen Army, provides a sterling example of this disregard of conventional gender norms.

Perolz was one of the many women sent down the country to deliver messages in the confusion and chaos of Easter Sunday. Would there or would there not be a Rising? The IRB had acted in secret, and consequently, when Eoin MacNeill cancelled manoeuvres for Easter Sunday, both sides reached out to Cumann na mBan to carry messages to straighten out the confusion. Perolz was sent from Dublin by Seán MacDermott to deliver messages about the Rising. She says: 'I was very proud to be sent on this mission' and she relates what happened as she tried to deliver a message to one member of the Volunteers:

> his wife said he was on night duty and he was now asleep. I said I did not care. I'd have to see him, and walked into his bedroom. That time we did not think about sex or anything else. We were all soldiers.[26]

It was quite a sensational act. Thinking of oneself as a soldier – not a woman soldier or a man soldier but a soldier. It was gender-defying.

Foster sees Perolz's statement as not necessarily an accurate one, but rather one which took on the sense, the flavour of the time at which she wrote it down: he says it 'may reflect the atmosphere of the 1940s and 1950s rather than the situation at the time'.[27] This certainly can be a problem with the witness statements, but they do give us an insight into

25 Senia Pašeta, *Irish nationalist women* (Cambridge, 2013), p. 133.   26 BMH, WS 246, Marie Perolz, p. 3.   27 Foster, *Vivid faces*, p. 127.

what women did and how they seemingly felt, especially those who did not keep diaries, letters or other written documents. Obviously, there is a class element encased here. Keeping a diary, writing letters and the like are activities of the middle class. Depending solely on these sources gives the research a middle-class bias.

However, there is also another issue to consider. Despite gender-norm-shattering acts, a pervasive patriarchal gender ideology operated deep in Irish as well as British society. In the beginning of the rebellion, perhaps even among some who led it, women and women's contributions were not taken seriously. To say it was a big mistake is an understatement. For example, the British army was disadvantaged because their troops believed that because the members of Cumann na mBan were female, they did not pose a threat. 'As multiple women recounted, it simply never occurred to most British soldiers that enemy combatants included women.'[28] Moreover, as one member of Cumann na mBan said in her witness statement: 'The British army did not know how to handle activist women. They often taunted revolutionary women with the threat "Don't think that just because you are a woman that I won't shoot you."'[29] But they did not.

After the Rising, the British army brought in female searchers to deal with women they suspected of carrying messages, arms or contraband goods of any sort. The women searchers, however, were few and far between. During the Anglo-Irish War, for example, Margaret Brady recalled how active her unit of Cumann na mBan was:

> By reason that we were girls, we [could] often get through the cordon while the enemy was carrying out roundups, where a man or boy could not, and it was easier for us to fool them. In this way, we were often able to get through to the column and the Volunteers, and tell them the enemy were coming so that they could hide and avoid being caught by surprise. It was very seldom that the enemy had lady searchers with them, and then only in very limited numbers. The girls were very keen on their work and got a good deal of enjoyment in foiling the enemy forces. Often they took revolvers and other arms from Volunteers during an encirclement roundup by

28 Karen Steele, 'When female activists Say I' in Gillian McIntosh & Diane Urquart (eds), *Irish women at war* (Dublin, 2010), p. 63.   29 BMH, WS 450, Brighid O'Mullane, pp 2–3.

the enemy and took them through the cordons to safety. Likewise, they regularly carried dispatches through the enemy lines.[30]

The witness statements abound with examples of young women destroying messages before they could be found by British forces, or carrying suitcases on trains filled with guns and ammunition, or ensuring that Volunteers escaped from raids while they themselves stayed behind to be harassed and arrested by British troops. For example, Eithne Lawless, who was secretary to Michael Collins at one point, remembered a police raid:

> At that stage we discussed what we were going to do. I think only Mick was armed. If any of the others were, the girls took the arms from them. I stuck Mick's revolver down my stocking and anything else incriminating, we girls took charge of. The police seemed to start the raid systematically from the bottom up thus giving us time to take these precautions. When they arrived, we had disposed of everything and they found nothing of any importance. They searched the men but not us.[31]

This situation, amazingly, carried on through the Anglo-Irish War, with women active in carrying dispatches and guns. Cal McCarthy, in his history of Cumann na mBan, asserts that 'overall, the British authorities were comparatively powerless in attempting to deal with female couriers'.[32]

Irish revolutionaries, both male and female, however, often fell prey to the same restrictive gender ideology. Again, the witness statements provide clues to their beliefs. Two examples will suffice: one member of Cumann na mBan missed the Easter Rising completely because another member did not think it was proper or suitable for a mother of three to participate in an armed rising. As Marie Fitzpatrick recalled in her witness statement:

> I was a member of Cumann na mBan. I was living in Bray when the Rising broke out. I walked in as far as Rathmines but could not get through the lines and had to walk back again. I got no

30 BMH, WS 1267, Margaret Brady, pp 7–8.   31 BMH, WS 414, Eithne Lawless, p. 2.   32 Cal McCarthy, *Cumann na mBan and the Irish Revolution* (Cork, 2007), p. 132.

mobilization order and when I asked Miss French-Mullen why, she said she would not bring me in on account of my three small children. I felt very disappointed over it as I had gone through all the first-aid and drill training.[33]

Not receiving mobilization orders was not uncommon. Another Cumann na mBan member, Leslie Price, remembered in her witness statement that she had not received mobilization orders on Easter Monday. She was waiting for such orders and finally an order came from Ned Daly 'to disband, go home, and await further instructions'. Price decided to ignore that order and go into the centre of the city. She explained Ned Daly's order by saying: '[Y]ou know the Volunteers, the kind of men they were: they thought we [women] should be away from all the danger.'[34] While the intention might have been good, the result demonstrated a restrictive gender ideology.

One of the most spectacular stories about joining the Rising belongs to Catherine Byrne/Rooney. She was urged to get involved in 1916 by her mother, who told her to follow her brother who had gone into Dublin's city centre. When she reached the GPO, she was refused admission. Undeterred by the refusal of a Volunteer to let her into the GPO and his threat of patriarchal retribution ('I'll tell Paddy [her brother] on you'), this determined young member of Cumann na mBan forced her way into the GPO. Catherine Byrne/Rooney seemed undaunted by the threat or power of the patriarchy. She went to a side street where she saw a Volunteer she knew – again we see the importance of radical geography. She relates how:

> The Volunteers had broken in the front window of the office, but the side windows had not yet been broken. I asked Frank Murtagh to lift me up to the side window … He did this with the aid of another Volunteer and I kicked in the glass of the window. I jumped in and landed on Joe Gahan …[35]

Needless to say, although she cut herself on the shattered glass, she was still able to perform first aid on a wounded Volunteer.

33 BMH, WS 1267, Margaret Brady, p. 6.   34 BMH, WS 1754, Leslie Price, p. 7.   35 BMH, WS 648, Catherine Rooney née Byrne, p. 2.

Another example from the witness statements regarding some women's eagerness to participate in the Rising, despite the operation of a restrictive gender ideology and the apparent confusion and indeed chaos of orders and countermanding orders, was the experience of Eva O'Flaherty. Volunteers and members of Cumann na mBan came from all over the country to Dublin to participate in the Rising, as the experience of Eva O'Flaherty demonstrates. She was from Kerry and was described as:

> [an] educationalist, entrepreneur, and Cumann na mBan activist, who cycled to Dublin upon hearing of the Rising – talked her way past the checkpoints surrounding the GPO. Her role, like her fellow Cumann na mBan members, was viewed by the rebel leaders as strictly non-combatants[36]

Despite this view of women as non-combatants, some women had weapons – at least the members of the Irish Citizen Army did. Constance Markievicz had a weapon and Helena Molony remembered James Connolly handing out revolvers to female members of the ICA while warning them not to use them except as a last resort.[37]

Regardless of whether they were prepared to take up arms or act in an auxiliary capacity, women saw themselves as part of the revolutionary movement. The Rising of 1916 gave them the opportunity to take whatever place they felt comfortable with on the arc of radicalization, which extended from the Rising through the Civil War. Visualizing women's participation as an arc gives a sense of mobility, fluidity and change. What women did in 1916 did not mean that this was what they would do in subsequent revolutionary periods. Or if they did nothing in 1916, it did not mean they would not be involved in the next stage of the fight for independence. Perhaps some women who participated in the Rising decided, for whatever reason, that these activities were not for them. Perhaps some wanted to participate more fully. There was no single formula.

Overall, however, women's participation in 1916 was important for three key reasons. First, it created a pattern, a template for women's

36 Bernard Kelly, 'Cumann na mBan: a Galway perspective' in Marie Mannion & Jimmy Laffey (eds), *Cumann na mBan: County Galway dimensions* (Galway, 2015), p. 7.   37 BMH, WS 391, Helena Molony, p. 33.

participation in revolutionary activities. Second, it established the fact that women were a vital part of the revolutionary movement and could command a place in the public sphere. By their actions in 1916, women who participated encouraged other women to do likewise.

Moreover, by their participation in the Rising, many women were radicalized. By radicalization, I mean that women were empowered, they became more independent and had a growing sense of equality. This is a contentious point among historians. A number of historians disagree. I argue that it was context that was important. To take but one example: it is one thing to make sandwiches in the privacy of your own home; it is quite another to do it in a burning building. Under the promise and protection of the Proclamation, undertaking private-sphere activities like cooking and first aid while bullets were flying and flames were dancing around very likely would have radicalized the women involved. They were choosing to risk their lives.

However, the people who perhaps were not radicalized or not radicalized in the same way or to the same extent, were some of the men of the Volunteers who continued to believe that women belonged in the home. To those who held firm to the ideology of domesticity, to these tenets of patriarchy, cooking meals – no matter where – was women's work. As Margaret Ward argues, in the eyes of many of the Volunteers, women were doing much the same thing outside the home as inside the home.[38] They never looked at the danger women were putting themselves in.

It was, moreover, not only individual women who were radicalized. Cumann na mBan evolved into a more self-conscious and independent organization in terms of their role in the struggle for independence. Tracing some of the changes in the constitutions of Cumann na mBan over the years of the revolution reveals not only the changes in this organization but also the differences in purpose, in the way that women saw themselves, and in their aims and ambitions.

As noted, the beginnings of Cumann na mBan are clouded in controversy. As is well-known, the Volunteers were founded in 1913 at the Rotunda Rink. It was lauded as an organization for men who would arm themselves and fight to defend Ireland. As Margaret Ward has pointed out: 'The Rotunda meeting was intended as a reaffirmation of the heroic spirit of Irish manhood.'[39] The meeting was an immediate success in terms of numbers and enthusiasm.

38 Ward, *Unmanageable revolutionaries*, p. 98.   39 Ibid., p. 90.

The role of women, however, was not clear. Pearse was the only speaker to mention that the Volunteers would be organized to defend the rights of Irishmen and Irishwomen, and that particular vision of equality, which would be echoed in the Proclamation of the Republic, did not seem to reflect the mood of the meeting.[40] Rather, the tenor of the meeting tellingly ignored that vision of equality and was contained instead in the phrase: 'There will be work for the women to do.'[41] That expression has echoed down historical corridors and certainly sounds less than inviting – perhaps even condescending.

Regardless of how you interpret this phrase, nationalist women took it as an opportunity to play an organized role in the advanced nationalist movement. Cumann na mBan thus came into being. At first it seemed that Cumann na mBan was to be a separate organization that would play an auxiliary role. According to its initial constitution, one of its main objectives was to raise money for arms for the Volunteers to use in the defence of Ireland.[42] It was an organization that was initially aimed at middle-class women who would be content to 'assist' the Volunteers. As Margaret Ward notes:

> The history of Cumann na mBan is, above all, an account of the tensions generated by this subordination and of the repeated attempts by some women to establish a greater degree of autonomy for themselves.[43]

Or as Cal McCarthy says in his work on Cumann na mBan:

> The gender stereotypes of the era meant that Cumann na mBan had identified for themselves a different role to that of the Volunteers.

---

40 Ibid.   41 In *Unmanageable revolutionaries* (p. 90), Ward maintains that while Pearse was the only person to mention women's rights, it did not satisfy Irish feminists, who were very conscious of the fact that women's right to citizenship was not included in the home rule bill. As we have seen, Pearse tried to remedy that in the Proclamation of 1916.   42 According to Lil Conlon, *Cumann na mBan and the women of Ireland* (Kilkenny, 1969), p. 8, Cumann na mBan had four objectives: to advance the cause of Irish liberty; to organize Irishwomen in furtherance of this object; to assist in arming and equipping a body of Irish men for defence of Ireland; to form a fund for these purposes to be called the 'Defence of Ireland Fund'. This same set of objectives appears in McCarthy, *Cumann na mBan*, p. 18.   43 Ward, *Unmanageable revolutionaries*, p. 88.

It was a role in which society had cast them and there is no doubt that feminists considered it an unequal one.[44]

In any event, the first meeting of the organization was presided over by Agnes O'Farrelly, a well-known figure in nationalist circles, but certainly not a firebrand. The historian Senia Pašeta claims that O'Farrelly was an 'attractive figurehead' who was selected to guarantee 'respectability' for those who questioned the propriety of women being involved in nationalist politics.[45] This interpretation is given additional credence when it is remembered that there is a parallel with the Volunteers, who installed Eoin MacNeill as a moderate front for the more radical forces of the IRB.

The origins of Cumann na mBan reveal the tensions surrounding women's participation in the public sphere. It was a contested issue. What we do know is that events would conspire to aid those nationalist women who wanted a more radical Cumann na mBan.

Like the Volunteers, Cumann na mBan split over Redmond's decision to embrace the First World War and urge the Volunteers to enlist.[46] The split in Cumann na mBan allowed the more separatist, radical nationalist elements of the organization to have more influence. For example, they now adopted a uniform and, while their numbers were small – one historian refers to them as a 'rump'[47] – this reorganized Cumann na mBan was to be closely aligned to the Volunteers and was to be characterized as a separatist, nationalist organization. In one of its manifestos, it declared that 'We feel bound to make the pronouncement that to urge or encourage Irish Volunteers to enlist in the British army cannot, under any circumstances, be regarded as consistent with the work we set ourselves to do.'[48] This sentiment would have squared nicely with the anti-recruiting campaign of Inghinidhe na hÉireann.

In fact, during this reorganization Inghinidhe would merge with Cumann na mBan en masse, and moderates like Agnes O'Farrelly left the organization. A new executive was formed including members such as Jennie Wyse Power. Indeed as the biographer of Jennie Wyse Power

---

44 McCarthy, *Cuman na mBan*, p. 134.   **45** Pašeta, *Irish nationalist women*, p. 134. The issue of respectability continued to plague Cumann na mBan in its subsequent recruitment drives. See below.   **46** For a discussion of the split in the Volunteer movement, see Charles Townshend, *Easter 1916* (London, 2006), see in particular, ch. 3, 'England's difficulty'.   **47** Matthews, *Renegades*, p. 108.   **48** Quoted from the Cumann na mBan manifesto, 5 Oct. 1914, in Matthews, *Renegades*, p. 108.

points out, 'By 1915, all their efforts were concentrated on the coming struggle for independence.'[49] One noticeable difference between the old and the new Cumann na mBan was the emphasis on military training – if not on shooting, then on the care and maintenance of weapons. This meant the women of Cumann na mBan would have a role in any armed struggle that would occur.

The subsequent constitutions reveal the thinking of Cumann na mBan and their attitude towards women's role in society. For example, in their constitution of 1919, the women of Cumann na mBan described themselves as an independent body of women pledged to work for the Irish republic.[50] Moreover, in outlining their policy aims for 1920–1, their first objective was 'To follow the policy of the Republican Proclamation by seeing that women take up their proper position in the life of the nation.'[51] Under the topic of political activities, Cumann na mBan documents also suggest that women undertake political work, adding that their members should keep 'before the public the fact that under the Republican Proclamation women were entitled to the same rights of citizenship as men' and recommending that members press for women candidates.[52] This, of course, would have the added benefit of allowing their male colleagues and the public at large to grow accustomed to women in the public sphere, in defiance of the traditional gender ideology.

Regardless of Cumann na mBan's evolution, one obvious and important point is that its very existence ruptured traditional gender norms. Taking this point in conjunction with the promise of equality given in the Proclamation and the opportunities presented in 1916 and in the Anglo-Irish War, traditional gender relations were challenged – not destroyed but destabilized. Women were taking risks or ignoring traditional norms and conventions. Marie Perolz, discussed briefly above, provides a sterling example of this disregard of traditional gender norms.

Another example of the way Cumann na mBan defied gender norms and challenged traditional attitudes toward respectability is given in the witness statement of Brighid O'Mullane, an organizer for Cumann na mBan. In her attempts to reach out to more women to join Cumann na mBan, she remembers that:

---

49 Marie O'Neill, *From Parnell to de Valera: a biography of Jennie Wyse Power* (Dublin, 1991), p. 81. 50 Military Pensions Collection, Military Archives, Cumann na mBan. 51 Ibid. 52 Ibid.

> I had a good deal of prejudice to overcome on the part of parents, who did not mind their boys taking part in a military movement, but who never heard of, and were reluctant to accept, the idea of a body of gun-women. It was, of course, a rather startling innovation and, in that way, Cumann na mBan can claim to have been the pioneers in establishing what was undoubtedly a women's auxiliary of an army. I fully understood this attitude and eventually, in most cases, succeeded in overcoming this prejudice.[53]

This comment is interesting for two reasons. First, it reveals that at least some women were willing to defy patriarchal gender norms. Second, it also demonstrates that some parents still clung to those traditional norms and ideals.

This second point is worth noting because, after the Anglo-Irish War and the Civil War, there was the establishment of a conservative Free State, which was very concerned about respectability, particularly women's respectability. Eillis Aughney, a prominent member of Cumann na mBan, who was anti-Treaty, wrote that 'the townsfolk, including our parents, were practically all hostile to Cumann na mBan because they adhered to the Republic'.[54] These would be some of the people who supported the Free State and, as Foster notes, favoured 'a reassertion of traditional attitudes ... [which was] a powerful theme in the history of the 1920s'.[55]

Cumann na mBan challenged this traditional gender ideology by giving women the opportunity to participate in the public sphere in a manner that could be interpreted as both a rejection of the ideology of domesticity and also as an extension of the domestic sphere. Because this could be interpreted both ways, it is perhaps one reason why the Volunteers were not radicalized as extensively as the women of Cumann na mBan. As Margaret Ward argues: from an average Volunteer's view, the women of Cumann na mBan

> were generally the sisters, wives and girlfriends of the Volunteers and whereas inside the home they washed, cooked and cleaned, outside the home they now sewed haversacks, learned first aid and raised money for the men. It was a division of labour that

---

53 BMH, WS 450. Brighid O'Mullane, pp 2–3.   54 BMH, WS 1054, Eilis Aughney, p. 4   55 Foster, *Vivid faces*, p. 7.

duplicated the differentiation of sex roles in the wider society and discouraged the expression of any alternative views.[56]

If true, this would be one reason why the ordinary Volunteer was very slow to be radicalized. Perhaps another was simply male privilege.

After the Rising, revolutionary women were active in different ways. With the execution of the leaders of the Rising and the mass arrest of men who were suspected of involvement in 1916, it fell to the women to pick up the pieces of the now tattered revolutionary movement – which they did, and did well. According to Kathleen Clarke, the work done by Cumann na mBan was of the upmost importance. 'They were women any country would be proud of and their courage and steadfastness were marvellous.' Clarke also mentions that the actions and attitudes of the women of Cumann na mBan, among others, helped to steady the country in a particularly trying time.[57]

One of the first concerns of the nationalist movement was for the families of the executed leaders of 1916 as well as the families of those who were imprisoned. Kathleen Clarke recalls that she had a certain amount of money, entrusted to her by the IRB, for the relief of the dependents of men engaged in the fight.[58] She founded the Irish Republican Prisoners' Dependants' Fund. Another fund was also started, the National Aid Fund, which, according to her memoir and her son's recollection, was composed 'largely of people hostile to the Rising, including Irish Members of Parliament'.[59] Eventually, the two funds were merged and worked together. One member of Cumann na mBan recalls 'how their task was the collection and distribution of money to aid the dependents of the thousands of prisoners who were deported to England where they were held until the end of the year'.[60]

---

56 Ward, *Unmanageable revolutionaries*, p. 98.   57 Kathleen Clarke, *Revolutionary woman*, ed. Helen Litton (Dublin, 1991), p. 133.   58 Kathleen Clarke was a well-known nationalist, a member of the Daly family from Limerick. She was an ardent separatist who was chosen by the IRB to be the keeper of their secrets, their money and their plans. She went anti-Treaty but later was active in the public life of the Free State. In 1939, she was elected the first woman lord mayor of Dublin. She was the wife of Tom Clarke and the sister of Ned Daly. *Revolutionary woman* is her autobiography.   59 Letter from Emmet Clarke, NLI, MS 44,041/7.   60 BMH, WS 805, Annie O'Brien and Lily Curran, p. 16.

Cumann na mBan, our branch included, was to collect money at church gates, [hold] flag days on the streets, ... We did the collecting and others were organized as distributors, who brought the money to the houses of those who were in need of it. This continued not only to the end of the year when the bulk of the prisoners came home, but also afterwards until the released men were in a position to support their families. There were also, of course, many families whose breadwinners were executed or killed in the Rising, which had to be helped for many years after.[61]

In addition, women also worked hard to preserve the memory of the executed leaders of the Rising. They were responsible for the propaganda that helped mould popular opinion in favour of the leaders of 1916. Women held them up as martyrs who should not only be remembered but venerated, thus joining Catholicism and nationalism. They organized a remembrance crusade with pictures and postcards, Masses of remembrance, and the publication of the prose and poetry of the dead leaders. The women not only insured that the leaders of 1916 would be remembered, they also raised the revolutionary fervour of nationalist Ireland. Such was their zeal that the British military commander was forced to admit to his government that there was a strong resurgence of feeling for the revolutionaries – and that it was due primarily to 'young priests and militant women – of them there seems to be a strong contingent'.[62]

Despite their brave work, some of the Volunteers and some of those in Sinn Féin were not really prepared to accept women in the public sphere. Many of those who would be the leaders of the Free State clung to their belief in the traditional domestic ideology, and to the belief that men should dominate the public sphere. This is an important point because it helps to explain how the Irish Free State evolved into such a conservative entity.

One telling event that demonstrates Cumann na mBan's concern over the Volunteers' possible lack of commitment to the 'equal rights and equal responsibilities' outlined in the Proclamation was the organization of the 1917 Sinn Féin convention. At this time, some nationalist

61 Ibid. 62 Quoted in Anne Haverty, *Constance Markievicz: an independent life* (London, 1988), p. 166.

women came together and voiced worries that women were in danger of being marginalized and indeed did not have proper representation on the expanding executive committee of Sinn Féin.[63] Calling themselves the League of Women Delegates, women from the Inghinidhe branch of Cumann na mBan, Cumann na mBan itself, the Irish Women Workers' Union and the Irish Citizen Army met to demand that women be given proper representation at any and all nationalist conventions.

They grounded their concern in their belief in the Proclamation of the Republic. At their meetings, in their letters and in their resolutions, they began by citing this iconic document. For example, in a resolution proposed by Jennie Wyse Power, seconded by Miss Molony and carried unanimously, the League of Women Delegates stated that they were basing their request for adequate representation on the Sinn Féin executive committee on the Proclamation of 1916, especially on its guarantee of equal rights and opportunities for all its citizens.[64]

When they were unsuccessful in their claim, the executive of the League instructed their secretary to write to the Sinn Féin executive 'on the important question of the adequate representation of women on your Executive Council' and explain that:

> The claim of women to be represented is based mainly on the Republican Proclamation of Easter Week, 1916 ... The claim is also based on the risks women took equally with the men, to have the Irish Republic established and the necessity of having their organised co-operation in the further struggle to free Ireland, and the advantage of having their ideas on many social problems likely to arise in the near future.[65]

This quote encapsulates the main arguments women would use in the Free State in their advocacy of full citizenship. Women would cite the Proclamation, which, they believed, conferred legitimacy on their claims, would argue that they had earned their right to citizenship through their participation in the revolutionary struggle and that they brought a

---

63 Margaret Ward, 'The League of Women Delegates and Sinn Féin', *History Ireland*, 4:3 (Autumn, 1996), pp 37–41. 64 Minute books of Cumann na Teachtaire, Sheehy Skeffington Collection, NLI, MS 21,194 (47). 65 Letter sent from the secretary, League of Women, to the secretary, Sinn Féin executive, 1 Aug. 1917, minute books of Cumann na Teachtaire, Sheehy Skeffington Collection, MS 21,194 (47), NLI.

particular type of knowledge to solving social problems. This is important because, in this time of upheaval and regrouping, women's status was not clear. Nationalist women were concerned that equality and full citizenship would not be the concern of either the Volunteers or Sinn Féin.

This unease was borne out by nationalist women's dealings with Sinn Féin after the Rising. The women's appeal to be included in an expanded Sinn Féin executive was greeted with neither civility nor enthusiasm. They were not even given the courtesy of a reply. The women, therefore, had to march in a deputation to the Sinn Féin offices to receive an answer. As a result, they were granted four places on the expanded executive, not the six they had asked for or the number of places given to representatives of the released prisoners. However, their members took advantage of their positions on the executive to propose a very clever resolution: 'Be it resolved that equality of men and women in this organization be emphasized in all speeches and leaflets.'[66] As a resolution of the executive, it passed the convention, giving it special status that could be used by women to bolster their case for inclusion and equality.

One final note on this incident: the Sinn Féin convention of 1917 had chosen only twelve women out of more than a thousand delegates. As Margaret Ward notes in her article on the League of Women Delegates: 'The ordinary Sinn Féin member was not ready to have women represent his interests in this important meeting.'[67] This did not bode well for women's quest for citizenship. As noted above, it was nationalist men who were not radicalized in terms of gender.

The years 1917 and 1918 saw Ireland in turmoil. By-elections occurred throughout the country, with a split between the remnants of the Irish Parliamentary Party and Sinn Féin. There was the very real threat of conscription being applied to Ireland by a British government that could not or would not see what a tinderbox Ireland had become. There was, as well, the alleged 'German Plot', which saw massive numbers of bogus arrests as well as disruption to society. Through it all, Cumann na mBan continued to organize and grow.

66 Meeting of Sinn Féin executive, 25 Sept. 1917, minute books of Cumann na Teachtaire, Sheehy Skeffington Collection, MS 21,194 (47), NLI. 67 Ward, 'The League of Women Delegates and Sinn Féin', p. 40.

After the Easter Rising, Cumann na mBan had to reorganize. Kathleen Clarke left this description of her attempt to restart the Central Branch, Cumann na mBan:

> Miss Mac Mahon [Clarke's assistant] and I called a meeting of the members. ... It was a very stormy meeting. 'Where were you? Were you out? If not, why not?' were the questions bandied about. A motion was proposed that those who were not out in the Rising should be expelled; some members showed intense bitterness towards those who had not been out. I was in the chair, and instead of dealing with the motion I pointed out that the failure in most cases was due to the treacherous action of John MacNeill and his countermanding notice, which caused confusion and upset all plans. I said that the Rising was only the first blow, that the fight for freedom had to be carried on, and that our duty to Ireland and to our executed leaders was to close our ranks, forget our failures and get to work.[68]

Her advice was taken by Cumann na mBan members throughout Ireland. Working jointly on issues like caring for the dependents of those who were executed or imprisoned was probably helpful in bringing women together at this time. In Clarke's view: 'I often think of these women of Cumann na mBan and the Trojan work they did all over the country. ... This was not confined to Dublin, it was the spirit throughout the land.'[69]

As seems typical of nationalist women in general, and Cumann na mBan in particular, despite their work and their support for revolutionary activities, there continued to be a question about who they were and what their relationship was to the Volunteers and to Sinn Féin. In point of fact, there was definite overlap between the Volunteers and Sinn Féin. Cumann na mBan had worked hard during the by-elections to elect Sinn Féin candidates, but they felt they were in danger of losing their original purpose as a military organization. As a result they sought closer relations with the Volunteers. But there remained a doubt about their purpose, their status, their role in Irish society.

The historian Michael Laffan points out how some members of Sinn Féin saw Cumann na mBan as an auxiliary organization of Sinn Féin.

---

68 Clarke, *Revolutionary woman*, p. 133.   69 Ibid., p. 133.

Laffan believes that ordinary Volunteers were hostile to women's participation in politics. He says:

> There was much opposition to any involvement by women in the
> man's world of politics, and conservative, male-dominated bodies
> were suspicious of female self-assertiveness. The GAA requested
> the Sinn Féin standing committee to prevent the holding of 'flap-
> per' meetings throughout the country, and a copy of its letter was
> sent to constituency executives.[70]

Laffan further notes that 'in many districts Sinn Féiners practiced sexual segregation and separate women's clubs were established'.[71] This is
important because it reveals that at a time when women were supposed to
be full citizens of the state, according to the Proclamation, to which men
and women repeatedly swore allegiance, there still remained a question
of what women's relationship to the state would be. And it seemed that
proving themselves militarily was not enough, was not going to answer
that question in a positive manner.

While at their 1916 convention Cumann na mBan 'had formally
embraced their role in the Rising', this sentiment was elaborated on
in the following year when the organization pledged itself to the Irish
republic.[72] Furthermore, in 1917 the organization took upon itself the
responsibility for arming both themselves and the Volunteers. McCarthy
sees this as a 'revolutionary departure'.[73] However, it can also be seen
as an evolution – the evolution of an organization whose very existence
defied gender stereotypes, becoming more radicalized.

The question of women's role in the public sphere was a leitmotif
throughout this period. It certainly was up for discussion in the forth-
coming elections in 1918. It was particularly acute in the selection of
women candidates to stand for seats. As Kathleen Clarke recounts: 'I had
noticed that the present leaders were not over-eager to put women into
places of honour or power, even though they had earned the right to

---

70 Michael Laffan, *The resurrection of Ireland* (Cambridge, 1999), p.
203.   71 Ibid.   72 McCarthy, *Cumann na mBan*, pp 105–6. McCarthy claims that in
1917, Cumann na mBan proclaimed itself a feminist organization, reiterating its allegiance to the equality promised in the 1916 Proclamation. I am not at all sure that this is all
feminism was about at the time, but it certainly was a radical approach.   73 McCarthy,
Cumann na mBan, p. 106

both as well as the men had.'[74] In his book *The resurrection of Sinn Féin*,
Michael Laffan makes the point that there was a difference between local
Sinn Féin clubs and the national executive, which appeared to be more
welcoming of women.[75] Margaret Ward, on the other hand, takes quite a
different view of Sinn Féin in general. While acknowledging the distinction between local and national Sinn Féin, she concludes that Sinn Féin
in general 'remained what it had always been – a predominantly male
voice ... [which relegated women] to the political sidelines'.[76]

However, as the 1918 Representation of the People Act gave women
over the age of 30 the right to vote, it did seem like an appropriate time
to run women candidates. When pushed on this point, the Sinn Féin
executive hedged – ironically worrying about the legality of nominating
women. As Margaret Ward concludes, 'This hypocritical concern to be
law-abiding must have evoked cynical laughter from the women. In any
case, it completely contradicted the decision of the 1917 Ard-Fheis.'[77]
Sinn Féin was far from being a respectable political party which worried
about the legality of its activities. It endorsed – not to say embraced – the
1916 Rising, an event which was hardly legal. It nominated Volunteers
who were in prison as candidates. It vowed not to take its seats in the
House of Commons, but rather to establish an indigenous parliament.
Thus Sinn Féin's reply appears, as Ward states, hypocritical, an attempt
to use the issue of legality as a convenient excuse for maintaining male
political hegemony. Or on a much more straightforward level, perhaps
Sinn Féin officials did not believe women as a group could win. Rather
than say so, they either denied them the opportunity to run in desirable
constituencies or offered them constituencies they could not win.

In any event, there were at least four prominent women who were
interested in standing for election. Kathleen Clarke eventually did not
stand in 1918 because of some internal machinations and confusion
over whether she should stand in Limerick or Dublin, and neither did
Hanna Sheehy Skeffington. In the latter case, Hanna was offered two
constituencies in which to stand, constituencies that were not coveted
or even wanted by men. According to her biographer, Hanna refused to
accept this token gesture and believed there was no point in standing for
a 'hopeless seat'.[78]

74 Clarke, *Revolutionary woman*, p. 170. 75 Laffan, *The resurrection of Ireland*, ch.
6. 76 Ward, *Unmanageable revolutionaries*, p. 133. 77 Ward, *Unmanageable revolutionaries*, p. 134. 78 Margaret Ward, *Hanna Sheehy Skeffington* (Dublin, 1997), p. 226.

However, two women did stand for election: Winifred Carey, who was very involved in the labour movement and who had been James Connolly's secretary in the GPO, was nominated to stand in a Belfast constituency – a very difficult one – which she lost. Constance Markievicz was nominated in Dublin and won. As is well known, Markievicz was elected in Dublin and was appointed as minister for labour in the First Dáil government – the first woman minister. In discussing her nomination, she reputedly told Kathleen Clarke, who asked her how she managed it, that:

> she had to bully them: [she told them that she believed] she had earned the right to be a minister as well as any of the men, and was equally well fitted for it, educationally, and every other way, and if she was not made a minister she would go over to the Labour Party.[79]

By 1918, nationalists had beaten the Irish Parliamentary Party in a general election, established their own parliament, Dáil Éireann, appointed the first woman cabinet member, and had drifted into the Anglo-Irish War. The opening shots of the war are usually considered the ambush at Soloheadbeg, undertaken at the initiative of the local Volunteers. This was followed by the spread of a guerrilla struggle – to be termed the Anglo-Irish War – under the direction of Michael Collins. As in the Easter Rising, Cumann na mBan swung into action. Many of their activities were the same as in the Easter Rising. They cooked, they provided first aid, they acted as scouts and carried messages, ammunitions and arms – sometimes even smuggling rifles under their coats.

Because this was a guerrilla war, the stakes were higher and the fighting somewhat different. There were no central buildings occupied, like, for example, the GPO. Fighting was diffuse. Often the IRA struck a target and after a fight, retreated to the countryside. Some went on the run. Women were called upon to find safe houses for the Volunteers who were on run, help them mend and return them to the fight. As Margaret Lucey recounts in her witness statement: 'It was necessary for me at all times, day and night, to be on the alert for raids, hold-ups and searches by the British authorities in order to safeguard very vital

79 Sinéad McCoole, *Easter widows* (Dublin, 2014), p. 303.   **80** BMH, WS 1561, Margaret Lucey, p. 11.

documents.'[80] Women's houses were raided during the middle of the night when they were home alone with their children. They were terrorized by the British forces: there were charges of sexual assault and rape by the British forces.[81]

As British troops poured into Ireland, Cumann na mBan's services were invaluable. Once again, it was up to the women to pass through British blockades and undertake surveillance, warning the men of the IRA of troop movements and possible ambushes. The gender ideology that in 1916 discounted women's contributions was still in operation in the guerrilla war though. It would lessen as the war went on, however, and it is worth noting that when the Civil War broke out, Free State troops did not make the mistake of underestimating women.

Cumann na mBan women proved particularly able in documenting Britain's atrocities and setting forth Ireland's case for independence. They carried on the very important war of words – often on their own and usually under extremely difficult conditions. Their work certainly helped to persuade international opinion of the righteousness of the Irish cause and hence, in this sphere among others, contributed to the success of the IRA.

Recollections from the witness statements provide insights into the work of nationalist women in general and the women of Cumann na mBan in particular. Sometimes it was vital for the Intelligence Unit to employ nationalist women who were not part of Cumann na mBan and hence would not be suspected by the British authorities of aiding the IRA. For example, Dr Alice Barry remembered it was

> around October 1920, Collins who knew we were sympathetic to the cause had previously asked us to disassociate ourselves from Sinn Féin public politics and to keep our house as a refuge for dangerously wounded IRA men. ... [A]nother house that Collins used was the house of another Mrs Barry. Mrs Barry's daughter had a very fashionable and expensive hat shop in Stephen's Green where all the society people bought their hats and thus the house in Dun Laoghaire would be a safe one.[82]

81 For a discussion on this point see Matthews, *Renegades*, ch. 10, 'The war on women'. For a discussion on the terrorizing effect of raids by the British soldiers, see Clarke, *Revolutionary woman*.   82 BMH, WS 723, Alice Barry, p. 2.

Miss Annie Barrett was another example of a valuable asset who was told to limit her exposure. In fact, she was told to sever her ties with Cumann na mBan. She remembers it was early in 1919 when she 'was instructed by Liam Lynch, through Dan Hegarty who was then brigade vice commandant, Cork II Brigade, to discontinue my activities'. Her intelligence work was outstanding. She passed on telephone messages thwarting British plans and allowing the Volunteers to go on the run, to escape capture. Or sometimes she did not allow messages to go through at all, claiming that the lines were faulty. She believed this 'helped to delay the arrival of enemy forces and so helped the IRA to get away with captured arms'.[83] Another time, as she relates:

> In May 1919, I obtained particulars of a telephone message from Dublin to the British Forces at Fermoy informing them that some men who had been wounded in the rescue of Sean Hogan at Knocklong, were being accommodated in a house in the Michelstown area. I immediately passed this information by means of a telegraph messenger to the local [IRA] Intelligence Officer who relayed it to Battalion and Brigade Headquarters. The wounded men were removed before the British raided the house ...[84]

At the truce, she was officially attached to the Intelligence Branch of the 1st Southern Division.

Besides their work with the IRA, nationalist women of various hues also continued to be politically active on municipal boards and county councils, and as republican judges in Dáil courts. As republican judges, women implemented the law of the Dáil as the courts of the Irish republic supplanted those of the British. Moreover, nationalist women continued their work on local boards. For example, in 1920 there were four newly elected women on Dublin corporation – Jennie Wyse Power, Hanna Sheehy Skeffington, Margaret McGarry, and Anne E. Ashton.[85]

By the end of the Anglo-Irish War, there seems to have been a general recognition that women had played an admirable part in the independence struggle. Constance Markievicz, in her presidential address to the 1921 annual convention of Cumann na mBan, duly recognized the important work the organization had done. She said:

83 BMH, WS 1133, Annie Barrett, pp 3–4. 84 Ibid., p. 3. 85 O'Neill, *From Parnell to de Valera*, p. 119.

I say to you each and everyone how proud ... I was when I came
out of prison ... to hear tell of the great work Cumann na mBan
had done while I was in Mountjoy ... When the history of Ireland
is to be written the name of Cumann na mBan will be a name that
will go down to your children and your children's children and as
an organization will stand as a memorial to the Irish people as a
great organization of the past ...[86]

Markievicz was not alone in her evaluation of the role of women. Michael
Collins, the mastermind of the guerrilla war, speaking in July 1922, echoed Markievicz's sentiments when, in talking about women, he said:
'Few appreciate what Ireland owes to those who stood their ground during the first few years and no thanks that anyone can bestow on them will
be too great.'[87] Male appreciation of women's contribution was echoed
by Cathal Brugha, minister for defence during the Anglo-Irish War and
a cabinet opponent of Collins. He paid tribute to women for keeping
the spirit alive, for keeping 'the flame alive and burning'.[88] While male
nationalists applauded women's bravery, heralded their resistance to ter-
ror and indeed recognized their essential contribution to the military
struggle, it remained to be seen if this would translate to recognition of
women as equal citizens in the public sphere.

It did not happen. A truce was agreed to in July of 1921. The Irish
began negotiations with the British. The subsequent discussions resulted
in the Treaty of 1921–2 in which the Irish agreed to a limited form of
independence. The entire nationalist movement split over the Treaty,
including Cumann na mBan. After a poisonous discussion, Dáil Éireann
voted 64-57 in support of the Treaty. Civil war resulted, which brought
damage and destruction and, most significantly, the death of many on
both sides of the nationalist struggle.

Cumann na mBan appears to have gone overwhelmingly anti-Treaty.
Interestingly, both Ann Matthews and Cal McCarthy, in their respective
histories of Cumann na mBan, dispute the legitimacy of the vote – and
their objections are very probably correct. One of the prime concerns of
the anti-Treaty members of Cumann na mBan was maintaining allegiance

86 Quoted in Conlon, *Cumann na mBan*, p. 239.   87 Quoted in ibid., pp 263–4.   88 Beth
McKillen, 'Irish feminism and nationalist separatism, 1914–1923', *Éire-Ireland*, 17:4
(1982), p. 86.

to the republic, which they believed was founded on the Proclamation.[89] A meeting of the executive of Cumann na mBan in February 1922 voted 24-2 against the Treaty. Jennie Wyse Power, who had voted for the Treaty, resigned from the organization she had been instrumental in forming. The executive then called a convention of the various branches to decide the organization's view of the Treaty. The Treaty was rejected 'by a show of hands'. Anne Matthews claims that: 'This was the actual vote that determined the organization's position on the Republic versus the Treaty and the exact numbers have never been divulged.'[90]

Some members of Cumann na mBan drifted away, having little heart for the brutality and venom of civil war. Others, those women who supported the Treaty, for example, formed their own short-lived organization, Cumann na Saoirse (League of Freedom), which provided a platform for women to make their pro-Treaty views known. Once the fighting started, they undertook to provide assistance to wounded soldiers,[91] and some, it is claimed, acted as women searchers. But the climate of the times was against women's military involvement and, despite possibly aspiring to be like Cumann na mBan, the women of Cumann na Saoirse were absorbed by the political party Cumann na nGaedheal in 1923. With the exception of Jennie Wyse Power, who continued with political activism in the Irish Free State, most of the women of Cumann na Saoirse retreated into the domestic sphere. Interestingly, the Treatyite army made no provision for a women's organization.[92] The historian John M. Regan writes of a 'palpable misogynism within the ultra-conservative wing of the Treatyite regime',[93] a misogyny, I would argue, that found expression in the legislation of the Irish Free State.

The anti-Treatyite section of Cumann na mBan, however, was not deterred from military action and plunged into the fight. In many ways, they resumed their activities of the Anglo-Irish War. But this time it was different. The weapon of secrecy was missing, and former comrades recognized one another as players in this war and acted accordingly. As the historian Eve Morrison maintains, '[T]he widespread arrest and

89 BMH, WS 485, Brighid O'Mullane, p. 2. O'Mullane makes a point of saying that allegiance to the republic was considered an important point in the discussion surrounding the Treaty.   90 Matthews, *Renegades*, p. 319.   91 Ibid., pp 322–3; O'Neill, *From Parnell to de Valera*, pp 138–9.   92 John M. Regan, *The Irish counter-revolution, 1921–1936* (Dublin, 2001), p. 140.   93 Ibid.

detention of women by the pro-Treaty side during the Civil War was an implicit recognition of their military value.'[94]

The Civil War was not good to women. There were some high-profile women who publicly went anti-Treaty and who happened to be related to men who had sacrificed themselves for the republic. They were not treated kindly. For example, Mary MacSwiney and Margaret Pearse were characterized as hysterical, emotional and bitter. Their response was evaluated as personal, not political. It was assumed that their virulent opposition to the Treaty was rooted not in principle, but in the fact that their male relatives had died for the republic. These characteristics were then expanded and applied to all women who were anti-Treaty and used as an excuse to keep all women out of the public sphere and in the home.[95]

This interpretation ignores women's attachment to the promises of the Proclamation of the Republic and all that it meant in terms of 'rights and responsibilities' as well as citizenship and participation in the public sphere of the state. In their view, the pro-Treaty faction was ignoring the Proclamation and disregarding the republic, and thus they felt compelled to become the staunch defenders of the republic.

This point is often neglected in traditional histories of the period, which ignore the importance of the Proclamation of the Republic to feminist nationalist women. Because it promised equality in a society that exuded inequality and that denied full and unfettered citizenship to women, the Proclamation was very significant to many women. In her article on female republican activism, Eve Morrison noted that:

> It is important not to underestimate the significance of the 1916 Proclamation and women's participation in the Easter rebellion in providing female Republicans with the means to demand parity of esteem. The Proclamation gave nationalist women a language to assert their equality not previously available to them.[96]

94 Eve Morrison, 'The Bureau of Military History and female republican activism' in Maryann Gialanella Valiulis (ed.), *Gender and power in Irish history* (Dublin, 2009), p. 63. 95 In his book *Women of the Dáil: gender, republicanism and the Anglo-Irish Treaty*, Jason Knirck makes this argument and very interestingly points to other revolutions, especially the French Revolution, where this happened. I think you can make the argument that this is one cause of a multi-casual explanation for what happens to women in the Free State. 96 Ernie O'Malley, *The singing flame* (Dublin, 1978), p. 131.

As was pointed out earlier in this chapter, the promise and the language of equality made a distinct impression on the participants, especially the women participants, of 1916. They were citizens of the republic and hence entitled to act as its soldiers. Ernie O'Malley recounted a telling encounter that gives substance to this interpretation, from the early days of the Civil War, when the Free State soldiers set fire to occupied buildings:

> When flames ate through the houses, it was decided to evacuate O'Connell Street and a rear guard under [Cathal] Brugha was left to cover the retreat of the others. The girls had refused to leave. They recited the proclamation of Easter Week.[97]

Echoing some of the women of Easter Week who refused to leave burning buildings in 1916, in this battle in the Civil War, according to O'Malley, the women asked:

> Why, if men remained, should women leave? The question was debated with heat in rooms of burning buildings, under the noise of shells and the spatter of machine guns. Cathal Brugha had to exert his personal influence to make them go.[98]

Members of Cumann na mBan performed a variety of activities in aid of the republic. To quote Ernie O'Malley again, they performed an invaluable service:

> During the Tan war the girls had always helped but they had never sufficient status. Now they were our comrades, loyal, willing and incorruptible comrades. Indefatigable, they put the men to shame by their individual zeal and initiative.[99]

To give but one example: O'Malley speaks of Sheila Humphreys, a leader of Cumann na mBan, using her to provide an idea of what the routine of Cumann na mBan was:

> Dressed in uniform, she attended burials of our boys at the Republican plot in Glasnevin. She looked after our wounded,

97 Ibid.   98 Ibid.   99 Ibid., p. 148.

moving them from place to place; found safe houses for our
men to sleep in; guided strangers through the city, and carried
dispatches.[100]

Republican women, moreover, expanded their activities into new realms
– some of them even shooting at Free State soldiers, others, having been
arrested, going on hunger strike. In much the same way as in the Anglo-
Irish War, they were also responsible for propaganda against the activities
of the Free State.

Because anti-Treaty women became the staunchest defenders of the
republican cause, they were portrayed as rigid and uncompromising,
willing to shed more blood in pursuit of an ideal – the pure republic. For this, women were blamed for the Civil War.[101] The praise and
gratitude women had received for their part in the Anglo-Irish War had
changed to condemnation. The most notorious and egregious example of this is the pro-Treaty historian P.S. O'Hegarty, who wrote that
during the Civil War, Dublin was full of 'hysterical women' who were
'unlovely, destructive-minded, arid begetters of violence' and were
largely responsible for the bitterness and ferocity of the civil war[102] – a
position clearly not supported by the documents or the events of the
period.[103] However, the Civil War was such a devastating experience that
the need to scapegoat, to blame was enormous. Women were an easy and
obvious target.

In the end, the Civil War just drifted to a close. Liam Lynch was shot
dead. De Valera became the leader of the republican forces. Frank Aiken
gave the order to dump arms. It was over for republicans. For many soldiers who had fought against – and maintained the illegality of – the
Treaty, and especially the oath, their choice was stark: unemployment or
migration.

---

100 Ibid., p. 174. 101 For a discussion of this point see Knirck, *Women of the
Dáil*. 102 P.S. O'Hegarty, *The victory of Sinn Féin* (Dublin, 1924), p. 104. The noted
historian Maria Luddy very tellingly says in her foreword to Knirck's *Women of the
Dáil* that 'within a short period, the brave girls of the War of Independence had been
transformed into what P.S. O'Hegarty called the "implacable and irrational upholders of
death and destruction". It was, he declared, women who were largely responsible for the
bitterness and ferocity of the civil war.' 103 For a detailed discussion of the negotiations and discussions that occurred in the months prior to the Civil War, see my book
*Portrait of a revolutionary: General Richard Mulcahy and the founding of the Irish Free
State* (Dublin, 1992).

It was slightly different for women. As noted, women became associated with a virulent anti-Treaty stance,[104] and the narrative grew on both pro- and anti-Treaty sides that women polluted the public sphere and needed to be returned to the home. It was the triumph of the ideology of domesticity, an ideology to which both pro- and anti-Free Staters subscribed. This triumph of domesticity typified the climate of the newly formed Irish Free State and the conservative politicians who came to dominate it. As Regan points out: 'After the civil war there was a deep suspicion about the role politicized women had played in advancing the division of revolutionary Sinn Féin.'[105]

The legacy of the Civil War lingered on and many questions remained. How unconventional were those Irish revolutionaries who fought the War of Independence? Did they simply want freedom from England – a political revolution and not a social revolution? Were they, in fact, with notable exceptions, conservative revolutionaries? Should the contrast be between the radicalism of James Connolly, for example, and the conservatism of Kevin O'Higgins? O'Higgins was the popular face of the newly independent government and he boasted that he and his colleagues were 'probably the most conservative-minded revolutionaries who ever put through a successful revolution'.[106] It was an accurate appraisal. For the most part, it was the conservative element that dominated the new government and created a different world from the one imagined in the earlier revolutionary struggle.

The Cosgrave government and its followers came to be seen as a new elite. Foster argues that W.T. Cosgrave 'represented a new, managerial and potentially conservative element within the movement'.[107] But it was O'Higgins who was the most prominent player of what the historian John Regan called the 'counter revolution'. Regan sees O'Higgins as the dominant player in this new elite, which seemed to follow the old Irish Parliamentary Party rather than the revolutionary ideals. After Collins' death, both of these men became leading figures in the new Free State government and neither was a representative figure from the pre-revolutionary era. According to Foster: 'Such men represented a new wave of activists, detached from the visionary republicanism and cultural excitements of the pre-revolutionary era.'[108]

---

104 Regan makes this point also in *The Irish counter-revolution*, p. 140.   **105** Ibid., p. 140.   **106** John P. McCarthy, *Kevin O'Higgins: builder of the Irish state* (Dublin, 2006), p. 108.   **107** Foster, *Vivid faces*, p. 283.   **108** Ibid., p. 285.

The Civil War had a very clear, albeit negative effect, on men's perceptions of women's right to participate in the political life of the country.
It poisoned the narrative that women had a right to serve in the public
sphere and that they could contribute something vital to the building of
the state. This is important because it joined seemingly separate trends
together – the language of patriarchy, especially women-blaming, with the
language of nationalism, and the need to build a stable state. Moreover,
as has been noted, it contributed to the conservatism of those individual
Volunteers and members of Sinn Féin who were not radicalized during
the revolutionary period and were content with a conservative, traditional state.

It was not simply that the ideals of 1916 did not survive the revolutionary period. It was also that the Civil War made it imperative that the
government focus almost all of its energy on stability. Achieving stability
would overcome the government's – and especially O'Higgins' – fear of
'a spectacle of a country bleeding to death, of a country steering straight
for anarchy, futility and chaos'.[109] The Cosgrave government knew that
falling prey to chaos and confusion would simply prove the common
British assertion that the Irish were incapable of self-government, which
was 'long … a claim of anti-Irish racism'.[110]

In general, the Civil War weakened the political leadership and the
moral authority of the new state. It created such an air of uncertainty
that at the birth of the Irish Free State, the political leaders were not sure
if the state would survive, or if indeed it would bleed to death. This was
perhaps a particular horror of the Civil War. Not only was it a war against
former comrades, a truly gruesome experience in and of itself, it was also
a war that the government – especially the military leaders – knew that
the anti-Treaty forces did not have to win. All the anti-Treaty forces had
to do was inflict such damage on the new state that it would be unable to
function.

The anti-Treaty republican women of Cumann na mBan certainly
helped in the endeavour to bring down the state and played a noticeable role in carrying on the fight. However, the Treatyites prevailed and
the forces of conservatism triumphed. Civil war allowed the government
to move to the right and provided a justification for such a movement.
Under threat and looking for allies, it found the ideal collaborator in the

---

109 McCarthy, *Kevin O'Higgins*, p. 86.   110 Quoted in Aidan Beatty, *Masculinity and
power in Irish nationalism, 1884–1938* (London, 2016), p. 37.

Catholic church. The church was the perfect partner to the state. As O'Higgins' latest biographer commented:

> A government that was still wet behind the ears in the exercise of conventional authority appreciated clerical support. That appreciation would be manifested by an especially deferential attitude toward hierarchical opinion on various issues in the decade that followed. Indeed when most of the irregulars had turned constitutional and ultimately came to power in 1932, they [de Valera and Fianna Fáil] also persisted in that deference as a means of demonstrating their legitimacy.[111]

Thus, the Catholic church dominated Irish society with no countervailing organization to thwart its power or its hold on civil society. During the revolutionary period, there was a tension, an uneasy relationship between many of the advanced nationalists and the Catholic church as an official entity. In various encounters with the Gaelic Athletic Association, for example, the tension was evident.[112] The Gaelic League, moreover, also provided an opportunity for young nationalists to move beyond the strictures of the church as they cycled off to the west of Ireland to experience Irish College. Certainly, there were and remained individual priests who were sympathetic to advanced nationalist thinking, but on an organizational level, the Catholic church remained wary of such changes. The Civil War, however, changed all that, and the Catholic church embraced the Free State government and emerged in the new state as the dominant force in civil society. It promised order and stability. It condemned rebellion, and threatened eternal damnation to those who threatened to bring down the state – an impressive weapon.

The roaring '20s, the jazz age, the era of *carpe diem* seemed to pass Ireland by – at least officially. While the dominant discourse was rooted in traditional values and conservatism, feminism continued, socialism continued and challenges to the dominant discourse continued. Moreover, despite the conservative values preached by the Catholic church and embraced by the Free State government, issues that were defined as social problems continued to exist – issues such as venereal

111 McCarthy, *Kevin O'Higgins*, p. 92.   112 W.F. Mandel, 'The Gaelic Athletic Association and popular culture, 1884–1924' in Oliver Mac Donagh et al. (eds), *Irish culture and nationalism, 1750–1950* (London, 1983), p. 53.

disease, prostitution, unwanted pregnancy, birth control and abortion, not to mention the craze for foreign fashion, foreign dance and foreign music. All these remained a part of Irish life.

The Irish Free State turned to legislation to imbed inequality into the fabric of the state and ensure that the ideology of domesticity was part of the dominant discourse of the day. It was the Free State that compromised women's citizenship. It was the Free State that denied women the right to serve on juries, to work unimpeded in the civil service and in factories, to divorce, to use birth control, to overall be free and unencumbered citizens of the new state with the right to a place in the public sphere. It was the Free State that ultimately told women their place was in the home.

The promises of 1916 were no longer operative or relevant. The imagined community of Pearse and Connolly, the vision of the 1916 Proclamation, was no longer the ideal, the goal for which Irish statesmen and politicians would strive.

2

The first test of citizenship: jury service for women, or 'No women need apply'

It began in 1924. In that year the Irish government, the Cosgrave government of Cumann na nGaedheal, initiated its attack on women's public identity by introducing legislation that restricted women's right to serve on juries. While the debate was ostensibly about jury service, what was at issue was women's demand to participate in the public, political life of the country. It was the opening skirmish in what would be an ongoing struggle between nationalist feminist women and Free State politicians over women's post-revolutionary identity.

The decision on juries was prefigured by post-truce events. In 1924, the poisonous legacy of the Irish Civil War lingered on, shaping perceptions and influencing the contours of the new state. As Senia Pašeta points out, this emphasis on order and stability was typical of post-revolutionary states, and:

> The fragility of the advances won in earlier years became apparent as Irish feminists began to learn that a return to 'family' and 'traditional' values would be key components of the new state's determination to restore this stability.[1]

The new world of the Irish Free State seemed to be premised on the demise of revolutionary ideals. While certainly remnants of the ideas and ideals of the revolutionary period – of feminism, of socialism, of equality, of a fairer and more just society – remained floating through post-revolutionary Ireland, none of these were the dominant force. Feminism, for example, was kept alive by a relatively small group of women who consistently urged the government not to exclude women from public life, and not to introduce legislation that diminished their rights and whose

1 Pašeta, *Irish nationalist women*, p. 269. During the 1920s and 1930s, successive governments introduced a series of measures that deprived women of political and economic rights in the new state. A discussion of these legislative acts is at the heart of my book.

49

purpose, it seemed, was to keep them in the home. This, however, was not the era of gender concerns but the era of nationalism and nation-building coupled with blatant patriarchy.

In the main, post-revolutionary Irish society emerged as conservative, traditional and overwhelmingly Catholic, infused with male privilege. The promises of the 1916 Proclamation were swept aside. This foundational document, incorporating as it did the ideals of equal rights and equal responsibilities, was overwhelmed by disagreements, disputes and, often, petty quarrels. This became particularly apparent in the political events leading up to the establishment of the Free State. As noted, the truce of July 1921 ended the Anglo-Irish War. This was followed by intense negotiations and the proposal of the Anglo-Irish Treaty, according to the main terms of which the twenty-six counties would accept dominion status, and swear an oath of allegiance to the king, or face the threat of 'terrible and immediate war'.

Following a rancorous debate that seemed to portend the coming split in the revolutionary movement, in early January 1922, the Treaty was ratified in Dáil Éireann. The famed revolutionary leader Michael Collins, one of the negotiators of the Treaty, seemed to downplay expectations by accepting it as a 'stepping stone' to full freedom and independence. In his eyes, the Treaty could eventually be used to meet the aspirations of the Irish people.

In particular, Collins believed anti-Treaty feelings would be lessened if the Irish state adopted a republican constitution that distanced itself somewhat from the Treaty. That was a vital part of Collins' strategy. According to Foster, Collins' tactic was 'to try and preserve unity while drafting a constitution for the new Irish Free State that would be republican enough to reconcile the less extreme elements of the anti-Treaty party'.[2] To that end, he appointed a constitutional committee. What he wanted was a clear and concise document that was republican in orientation, which he believed would go some way to assuaging at least some of the anti-Treaty feelings. This document was not to be hampered by the terms of the Treaty. Collins wanted to convince his dissident colleagues of the value of the Treaty through quick, decisive and highly symbolic action – for example, watching British troops leave Dublin Castle.

What the government wanted was a vote to validate its position on the Treaty. They wanted to go to the Irish people and ask them to vote

2 R.F. Foster, *Modern Ireland, 1600–1972* (London, 1988), p. 509.

for or against the Treaty. This was important because, if passed, it would then have the strength of being a democratically accepted document and provide the government with a mandate for implementation. Pro-Treaty officials believed there was a great deal of support in the country for ending the war with Britain and accepting the Treaty. They wanted this acknowledged.

It was complicated, however. It was not even clear who would vote in these elections. The current electoral register was hopelessly out of date. For example, on the issue of women's suffrage, the 1918 Representation of the People Act gave the vote only to women over the age of 30. That meant numerous younger people, especially members of Cumann na mBan, who were known as being notoriously anti-Treaty, would be excluded from the vote. The common belief was that it was the younger people who were more anti-Treaty, perhaps more rebellious. Moreover, in accord with the spirit of the Proclamation of 1916, any upcoming vote for ratification or otherwise should have been based on universal suffrage.

Although a deputation of women suffragists, including Hanna Sheehy Skeffington, met with Griffith and de Valera to discuss the idea of an extension of the franchise, of revising the electoral register, it was all to no avail. The women estimated that it would take approximately three months to complete a revision of the register. The request was declined. Griffith saw it as simply a ploy to delay the acceptance of the Treaty. The matter was later brought up in the Dáil on 2 March 1922 by Kate O'Callaghan but it was defeated.[3]

This, however, did not deter Collins – and eventually Griffith – from agreeing to a pact with de Valera that included a three-month delay in the election. One reason for the delay was the fear of a split in Sinn Féin throughout the country that might prevent an election from happening. Another was to give the constitution a chance to be completed so that the Irish people would have a clear idea of what they were voting for. The important point is that an outdated register which excluded a large number of those who had fought in the Anglo-Irish War was not deemed an important enough reason to postpone the election, especially because it involved the issue of women's suffrage.

The Collins-de Valera pact was the triumph of patriarchy, of patriarchy over democracy, of patriarchy over feminism, of patriarchy over the promises of 1916. Patriarchy by its very definition is the rule of older

3 Ward, *Unmanageable revolutionaries*, pp 174–275.

men over younger men and over all women. For their own reasons, neither de Valera nor Collins saw it in this light.

To put it a different way: the period from the signing of the Treaty
to the outbreak of the Civil War can be characterized as the triumph
of nationalism over all other concerns. The nationalist objective in these
pacts and agreements was to ensure that unity prevailed. For example,
Collins' overall aim was to keep the revolutionary movement, especially
the army, together. While Collins acknowledged the importance of a general election to allow the Irish people to vote on the terms of the Treaty,
he compromised his position in the interest of unity with the Collins-de
Valera pact, which delayed the election for three months.

To Collins, the most important objective was to avert a split in the
nationalist movement and prevent the opponents of the Treaty from
gaining power. As the historian Joe Lee has pointed out, both pro- and
anti-Treaty sides were broken down into moderates and extremists.[4]
Thus it made sense for the moderates on both sides to make a pact, for
Collins to make a pact with de Valera. To forestall the drift to civil war,
Collins agreed to delay the election for three months and promised a
cabinet that would reflect the current strength of the opposing sides in
terms of ministers. In delaying the election for three months, the pact
did what Griffith and Collins refused to do to update the electoral register. Nationalism triumphed yet again.

Collins also seemed to promise a republican constitution. In reality,
his assurance was premised on the belief that the constitutional committee would produce a constitution that the British would accept, but was
also republican in spirit and not actually tied to the Treaty. If he could
work this magic, Collins believed the nationalist movement would survive and civil war would be avoided. Unfortunately, there was no magic
in the constitution of 1922.

The constitution that first emerged from the committee basically
ignored the Treaty and hence was not acceptable to the British. In an
updated version, the Treaty transitioned to be included in the constitution of 1922. In a boorish move, the British took a Shylockian view
of the Treaty. Demanding their pound of flesh, the British insisted that
the Irish abide by the letter of that document. It did not seem to matter
that the provisional government was facing a realistic possibility of civil
war or that the demand of the British that the Irish be forced to stay

4 J.J. Lee, *Ireland, 1912–1985: politics and society* (Cambridge, 1989), p. 57.

in the empire/commonwealth contradicted their dealings with the other dominions. The British forced the Irish constitution into the straight-jacket of the Treaty. Despite Collins' hope that the constitution be based on popular sovereignty and be 'republicanish', it became a document that did nothing to ease the tensions raging in Irish society. No one could really be surprised when civil war broke out in June 1922.

The constitutional committee had initially convened in early 1922 and met from January through June. Michael Collins was the titular head, but his multiple roles in government and the army precluded him from active participation as chair. That role fell to Darrell Figgis, a noted literary figure, a disciple of Arthur Griffith and an active figure in the Volunteers. The remainder of the committee was made up of lawyers, a business man, a civil servant and two academics. No woman sat on the constitutional committee. As the legal scholar Thomas Mohr points out concerning the deliberations on the constitution: 'It was overwhelmingly a story of men discussing the rights of women.'[5]

Despite this glaring omission, it seems that, taking a cue from the Proclamation of 1916, there was an equality provision.[6] While the constitution of 1922 has not received the attention and analysis of its successor, the constitution of 1937 (Bunreacht na hÉireann), its repu-tation tends to centre on its equality clause. Originally, it was a very full rendition of equality, but it was cut numerous times, rearranged in various articles that finally became article 3 of the 1922 constitution. It read: 'Every person without distinction of sex, domiciled in the area of the jurisdiction of the Irish Free State ... is a citizen of the Irish Free State ... and shall within the limits of the jurisdiction of the Irish Free State ... enjoy the privileges and be subject to the obligations of such citizenship.' It seemed clear at the time – especially to various nation-alist women – that, for example, restrictive legislation that prevented women from sitting on juries violated article 3 of the constitution of the Irish Free State.[7]

It is not clear why the equality clause was pared down numerous times. It seems it did not fit, in a natural way, with any of the other clauses – did not fit or wasn't seen to fit. Perhaps the equality clause was pared down simply to make the document shorter. Perhaps some actually believed it

---

5 Thomas Mohr, 'The rights of women under the constitution of the Irish Free State', *Irish Jurist*, 41 (2006), pp 20–59.   6 Laura Cahillane, *Drafting the Irish Free State con-stitution* (Manchester, 2016), pp 90–2.   7 *Irish Times*, 22 Feb. 1927.

was not necessary. Alternatively, perhaps it was done as a reaction to the growing anti-women feeling intensified by the Civil War.

Moreover, there is a mystery about women and the constitution as reported by the legal historians Laura Cahillane, in her book *Drafting the Irish constitution*, and Thomas Mohr, in his article 'The rights of women under the constitution of the Irish Free State', published in the *Irish Jurist*. Mohr alleges that during the debate on the constitution, 'a deputation of women called to government offices to discuss the equality provision with members of the provisional government'.[8] These women remain unidentified. Given the conditions and divisions in the country, I would suggest that these were pro-Treaty women but not members of Cumann na mBan – or maybe prominent conservative women who had no interest in an equality clause.

According to Mohr, the unidentified women suggested that a strong equality guarantee could be used to render unconstitutional any legislation that discriminated between the sexes. Cosgrave's alleged response that this would create 'endless bother' seems to provide an air of legitimacy to a mysterious meeting that is known only through O'Higgins' uncorroborated account.[9] If true, it is borne out by the subsequent actions of Cosgrave, O'Higgins and the provisional government. Perhaps it was floated by O'Higgins as a justification for the anti-feminist, at times anti-woman, attitude of the Cumann na nGaedheal government.

With the establishment of the Free State, the Cosgrave government began the process of state-building, of filling in the contours of the new state. It was the responsibility of the government to implement the implicit commitment to equality set out in the constitution. What became apparent was that the Cosgrave government – and its successor, the de Valera government – foresaw no public role for women. Women had a domestic but not a political identity. Women were mothers. Women were wives.

Obviously, this was a massive retreat from the beliefs of Inghinidhe na hÉireann, from the promises of 1916, indeed even from the spirit of the constitution of 1922 – nationalist feminist women had entered the Free State with expectations of full citizenship. Those who had supported the Treaty and hence, after 1922, supported the Cosgrave government and the Cumann na nGaedheal party, believed that they had achieved political

8 Mohr, 'The rights of women', p. 30. 9 Ibid., p. 30; see also Cahillane, *Drafting the Irish Free State constitution*, p. 92.

equality through the constitution of 1922. That is obvious because in debates over legislation that curtailed their rights, women accused the government of violating their own constitution.[10] They thought their role in the new state would incorporate more than simply a domestic identity. They trusted the government, most of whose members had been colleagues and comrades, to hold to the promise implicit in the independence struggle, of equality, of a state that guaranteed 'equal rights and equal opportunities to all its citizens' and cherished 'all of the children of the nation equally'.[11] They were disappointed and believed that their trust had been misplaced.

Alternatively, those feminist nationalist women who were anti-Treaty were bitterly opposed to the Cosgrave government and distrusted its motives and intentions. The gendered legislation the government introduced simply confirmed their worst fears. These women supported de Valera and the Sinn Féin party, although there was a certain wariness among some of them about their male colleagues' views on gender issues.[12] Hanna Sheehy Skeffington, for example, referred to de Valera as a conservative, Church-bound anti-feminist.[13]

During the 1920s, a number of women's groups resurfaced. Some of these had recast themselves after suffrage had been won. The Irish Women's Citizens and Local Government Association, for example, was founded in 1920 and was the successor to the Women's Suffrage Association. Among its objectives was 'to watch legislation affecting women and children'.[14] There was also the Irish Women's Equality League, formed for the protection of women's interests, as well as the Women's International Peace and Freedom League. In 1924, an umbrella organization, the National Council of Women of Ireland was established 'to promote joint action among women's organizations in Ireland and to stimulate thought and cooperation on all questions of social interest'.[15] The issue of jury service for women galvanized these groups into action.

10 This is true of the juries bills analysed in this chapter, as well as bills in ch. 3.   11 Proclamation of the Republic, 1916.   12 In an undated letter (*c.*1932?), Hanna Sheehy Skeffington wrote: 'I have no belief in de Valera. Well meaning, of course, better than Cosgrave, but really essentially conservative and Church-bound, anti-feminist, bourgeois and the rest. A sort of professor-type, like Wilson, and enamored of phrases and abstractions.' Hanna Sheehy Skeffington Papers, MS 24, 134, NLI.   13 Ibid.   14 Testimony before the Committee on Vocational Education, MS 941, vol. 20, NLI.   15 Ibid.

The juries amendment bill of 1924 arose out of a governmental conference. While there was consensus that a general reform of the jury system would be necessary at some later date, the bill that emanated from the conference centred on procedures and methods relating to jury service. However, the conference concluded that a few issues were 'of such urgency and importance' that they had to be included. One of these issues was the 'exemption of women jurors on application'.[16] This section was included in the bill 'pursuant to verbal instruction from the Ministry of Home Affairs'.[17] While retaining women's right to serve on juries, the bill gave them exemption upon demand. Just by notifying the appropriate official, women – simply because they were women – would be excused from jury service with little or no difficulty. The minister for home affairs, Kevin O'Higgins, stated that one of the purposes of the 1924 bill vis-à-vis women was 'to get rid of the unwilling woman juror'.[18] Of the unwilling male juror, nothing was said.

Claiming that the number of women who wished to serve on juries was 'very small', the minister contended that 'the insertion of women's names in the Jury Book leads to nothing but trouble; the women do not turn up, or they get themselves excused, or they are objected to'.[19] The government therefore felt it had no choice but to acknowledge the reality that the 'woman juror has not been an outstanding success'.[20] The minister for home affairs went on to say that:

16 Memorandum to the executive council from the minister of home affairs, 19 Feb. 1924, NA, Ministry for Justice Files, H171/35. 17 Ibid.; Kennedy Papers, P4/1181, UCD Archives. The idea of exempting women on demand was favoured by (if not originated by) Mr Lorcan Sherlock, sub-sheriff in Dublin, who was part of the governmental conference on reform of the jury system. In a memorandum from Attorney General Hugh Kennedy to Minister of Home Affairs Kevin O'Higgins of 3 Dec. 1923, Kennedy wrote: 'I know that amongst other ideas Mr Sherlock had, he thinks that women jurors should not be put on the list unless on their own express application. I should have though that this proposal would meet with feminist opposition. I was however surprised a few days ago when a deputation from a feminist society which came to me with reference to the judiciary bill, expressed their hearty approval of Mr Sherlock's suggestion'; NA, Ministry for Justice Files, H171/35. This is the only reference I have found to a feminist group supporting the exclusion of women. I have not been able to identify it nor do I know if this group subsequently changed its mind. I could find no major feminist group that publicly supported the 1924 bill. 18 *DD*, 5 Mar. 1924, vol. 7, col. 1664. 19 Ibid. 20 *DD*, 13 Mar. 1924, vol. 7, cols 2095–6.

The proposal that we are putting forward is that any woman who has a taste for that service, any women who wants to serve on juries, is perfectly free to do so, but we do set out the fact that there are a great many women who abhor that service, and we do not propose to drag unwilling women into jury boxes in response to the claims of a certain number of their advanced sisters – a small number.[21]

It was, according to O'Higgins, the responsibility of 'the advanced ladies to convert their less advanced sisters'.[22]

O'Higgins set the tone of the argument in the Dáil. He believed that women did not want to serve on juries and, therefore, women should not have to serve on juries. The most efficient way to deal with their reluctance was to allow them to opt out. However, beyond that, O'Higgins also claimed that men were different from, not to say superior to, women. Speaking in the Dáil, the minister said:

But men have not that shrinking from the duty, that reluctance to go into the box and face the ordeal of sitting for perhaps four, five or six days trying a man for his life than the normal woman has. A few words in a Constitution do not wipe out the difference between the sexes, either physical or mental or temperamental or emotional ...[23]

It was a bald statement of male superiority.

Certain important and recurring themes began to appear during this discussion on jury service. Throughout the debate, those who supported the government's position pictured women not only as unwilling to serve on juries but also as incapable of dealing with the responsibilities of citizenship. Women were described as 'frightened out of their lives at the idea'[24] of serving on juries, as approaching it 'with the utmost dread', because a number of them were 'quite unfitted for it'[25] or were 'sensitive, nervous ... with a positive reluctance and a distaste for this service'.[26] It was not a flattering picture, nor one which held out much hope that women would be seen by the political establishment as having a public identity.

21 Ibid. 22 *DD*, 13 Mar. 1924, vol. 6, col. 2096. 23 *DD*, 15 Feb. 1927, vol. 15, col. 489. 24 *DD*, 13 Mar. 1924, vol. 6, col. 2097. 25 Ibid., col. 2098. 26 Ibid., col. 2103.

Significantly, supporters of the legislation began to make the link between domesticity and normalcy, between desiring to stay in the home and being a 'real' woman:

> We also know that the normal woman will have no desire or anxiety to serve on a jury and she never will serve on a jury if she can avoid it. ... The normal man is prepared to accept this responsibility in that respect. ... the jury box is not the place for the normal woman, and that the normal woman will never find her way into that box if she can help it.[27]

Indeed, deputies made the point – which would become more explicit and contextualized slightly differently in 1927 – that 'the neurotic women shall serve on juries because they may desire to serve on juries. ... they are not the type of women that you should urge or even allow to serve on juries to the exclusion of normal women'.[28]

Needless to say, women's groups were far from pleased with this legislation, viewing with 'alarm the proposal ... to exempt women on the ground of sex alone'.[29] The Irish Women's Citizens and Local Government Association passed a resolution, which it sent to every member of the Dáil, protesting 'that women have no right to evade the duties and responsibilities involved in citizenship' and pointing out that to allow women to do so just because they were women was 'unfair to the men citizens and derogatory to the women'.[30]

Feminists rejected the contention that women were frightened of jury service:

> Now this chivalrous sex, ever eager to conduct us through what is, in its opinion but not always in ours, a difficult situation, has been allowed to persuade itself that we want to get out of serving on juries. You will notice that it has arrived at this conclusion all on its own. ... I suggest that this shying before jury service is all a man-made myth.[31]

Women's groups did acknowledge that some women had imposing domestic responsibilities. These women could be excused from serving

---

27 Ibid., col. 2101. 28 Ibid., col. 2103. 29 Letter to the editor, *Irish Times*, 10 Mar. 1924. 30 Letter to the editor, *Irish Times*, 12 Mar. 1924. 31 Letter to the editor, *Irish Independent*, 29 Apr. 1924.

on juries. It was not a question of forcing mothers to abandon their young. The Irish Women's Citizens and Local Government Association pointed out that 'women under the present system have no difficulty in obtaining exemption for valid reasons, such as having small children to care for or other domestic duties'.[32] In fact, some characterized the government's pronouncements about women's responsibilities in the home as mere sentimentality:

> And then the Family. They went one better on that wonderful, ephemeral entity. It dribbled sentiment into the most stolid fountain pens. For the time being this institution was receiving more attention that the rarest orchid. On paper, of course. It is about the only way in which it does get attention from many of the dear old chaps.[33]

For many women, the 'sanctity of the family' argument rang somewhat hollow.

Women's groups were quite clear about the importance of the issue at stake. Describing the bill as a 'retrograde step', they urged

> upon women very strongly the necessity for seeing the dangerous tendency in grandmotherly legislation of this description. If this proposal were to become law, it would open the door a little wider to the forces of reaction, and women may see their power for good, which they have so hardly attained, being generally nullified.[34]

The consequences of this legislation would be dire. Feminists predicted that it would be 'discouraging to civic responsibility' and was not in the 'best interest of women or the community as a whole'.[35] Women now had a share in the government and as such had a duty to understand the conditions in the country. Jury service would help women acquire that knowledge.[36]

Despite these arguments, the government prevailed. Once the legislation was passed, the government gave it very wide publicity.

32 Letter to the editor from the Irish Women's Citizens Association, *Irish Times*, 12 Mar. 1924. **33** Letter to the editor, *Irish Independent*, 29 Apr. 1924. **34** Letter to the editor, *Irish Times*, 10 Mar. 1924. **35** Ibid. **36** Letter to the editor, *Irish Independent*, 29 Apr. 1924.

Announcements were put into the newspapers advising women as to the procedure for applying for an exemption. In fact, after some discussion, the government decided to mail exemption cards to eligible women.[37] The results of the legislation were predictable. In County Dublin, for example, the number of exemption forms issued to women jurors was 4,514. The number of applications received was 3,339, and of these, 3,276 were approved. The number of names of women who would appear in the jury book totalled 1,238. In County Mayo, the figures, on a much smaller scale, were similar. Of 482 women who were sent exemption forms, 435 applied for exemptions and only 47 names remained on the register.[38] Of those who did opt to participate in the jury system, few women were empanelled, and fewer served.

The situation was not allowed to rest at exemption on demand for women. As early as 1925, a memorandum was circulated in the Justice Department that suggested removing women completely from jury service: 'The woman juror is abolished. The 1924 Act gave the woman exemption if she so desired. The few who remain are not worth catering for and are not in fact useful jurors.'[39] Despite the fact that there were complaints about the lack of male jurors, that indeed a judge in Dublin was forced to suspend proceedings because of an inability to field a jury,[40] despite the fact that it seemed as if there was such a shortage of male jurors that indeed Kevin O'Higgins was forced to go on record as promising that no eligible juror in Dublin would be called upon to serve more than once every three years,[41] despite all of this, it seemed as if the government would not give the 1924 system a chance to work, but rather was intent on doing away with the woman juror.

This fact was cloaked in a number of half-truths. The government held that women did not want to serve on juries and the small number who did was proof of this. Apparently, however, the small number could have been due to a number of other reasons. During the debate on jury service, Hanna Sheehy Skeffington enlightened the discussion with a startling fact: women were not serving on juries because they were not actually called upon to do so and, importantly, the number-one offender

---

37 'Implementation of Juries Act, 1924', memorandum from the minister of local government, 27 Mar. 1924, NA, Ministry of Justice Files, H171/35. 38 Ibid. 39 'Memorandum to accompany departmental rough draft of the juries bill, 1925', Ministry of Justice, File 284/3, NA. 40 'Dublin Letter', *Cork Examiner*, 30 Apr., 1925. 41 Ibid., Nov. 16, 1925.

in these cases was the government itself. In a lengthy letter to the *Irish Independent*, published in November of 1925, she wrote:

> The fact is that no women are allowed to serve on juries and for nearly two years an elaborate system of camouflage has gone on by which the authorities themselves connive at the breaking of the law which allows women to serve as part of their rights as citizens.
> ...
> Then Mr O'Higgins and his advisors were faced with a dilemma. Had he had his way he would have excluded all women from juries, but this would have involved fresh legislation and possible opposition from various quarters. His only other alternative was to exclude those [women] who did not claim exemption and this has been done by applying to women the same methods formerly used to disqualify Catholics in the old days of jury packing.

The result, according to Skeffington, was that:

> [W]omen are now summoned and when their names are called, the State in virtue of its right of unlimited challenges, orders them to 'Stand By'. They have, however, to remain in court ... In Green Street last week, I saw several women waiting for hours, having been told to 'Stand By' but not dismissed ...
> In view of the repeated wails of judges and sheriffs as to the scarcity of jurors ... [why was the Free State preventing women from serving on juries?] When I inquired as to the reason why the Free State authorities thus debarred women willing to act from jury service, I was informed by an official that Minister for Justice feared that women 'would be unwilling to convict' in certain cases.[42]

Given the state of the country, even post-Civil War, when outrages were not uncommon, this was definitely a concern for the minister. Sheehy Skeffington thought it 'sinister'.[43] It certainly bespoke a particular world view.

42 Letter to the editor from Hanna Sheehy Skeffington, *Irish Independent*, 17 Nov. 1925. 43 Ibid.

Other reasons, however, also emerged. It was later claimed that the members of the legal profession as well as those set to stand trial did not want women jurors. They believed that women 'made up their minds too soon, and that all the arguments of the best advocate could not alter that'.[44] Moreover, there was a concern that women, especially if pretty and wearing short skirts, would be likely to 'distract the minds of the other jurors from a mature and careful consideration of the evidence'.[45] It is amazing that, if this last reason were true, if men were so easily distracted, they were allowed to serve.

As Hanna Sheehy Skeffington had predicted in her 1925 letter, quoted above, it would take a new bill to exclude women altogether – and this bill would spur opposition from women's groups. She was prophetic. In 1927, the Cosgrave government proposed the rather extreme step of removing women from jury service altogether. Asserting that the 1924 bill was 'simply ludicrous in its results',[46] the government claimed that, because most women applied for exemptions, it was an unnecessary burden on the state for its officials to draw up jury lists which included women and then be forced to keep a record of exemptions and non-exemptions. Administrative efficiency and financial savings demanded that a change be made. According to Ciara Meehan's very favourable estimation of Cosgrave and his government, efficiency was a key factor in the Cumann na nGaedheal government's decision-making process. She wrote: 'Focus was placed on introducing legislation that not only sought to strengthen the structures of the state, but also aimed at increasing efficiency.'[47] The issue of efficiency was a useful and effective cover for the gender ideology that clearly emerged during these debates.

Once again, it was the minister for justice, Kevin O'Higgins, who articulated the government's position. According to the minister, the situation was simply that 'the great bulk of the women of the country are unwilling, most reluctant, to serve on juries'.[48] It was, therefore, simply an unnecessary administrative expense – 'not good business', 'not reasonable' – to list women as potential jurors only to have them remove their names.[49] It was particularly bad financial and administrative

---

44 This quote came from the Seanad debate in 1927 but it was also expressed in newspapers of the period. *SD*, vol. 8, 30 Mar. 1927, Mr O'Farrell, cols 677–8.   45 Ibid.   46 *DD*, vol. 18, 15 Feb. 1927, col. 489.   47 Ciara Meehan, *The Cosgrave party: a history of Cumann na nGaedheal* (Dublin, 2010), p. 29.   48 *DD*, vol. 18, 15 Feb. 1925, col. 468.   49 *DD*, vol. 18, 15 Feb. 1927, col. 467.

strategy because women's participation on juries, in O'Higgins' view, was not really necessary: 'The machine will work without compelling the woman juror to come forward. We can, without undue hardship on the eligible male population, keep the courts served with juries.'[50] Moreover, not only were their services not necessary, the minister contended that indeed women jurors presented distinct problems:

> [T]here are difficulties surrounding the question of jury service for women that are not involved in the question of jury service for male citizens [bathroom facilities, for example]. In effect, in this Bill of mine the State takes the view that the woman juror presents difficulties that make the service that one could secure thereby administratively not worthwhile.[51]

The 1927 bill, O'Higgins asserted, would thus save the state money and make its operations more efficient. Although he could not say exactly how much money would be saved or how much time would be freed, the minister argued that, as the total number of women jurors in 1925 was about 40, keeping them was clearly not worth the effort. It was not that he thought that women were 'incapable of rendering reasonably good service on juries ... probably as good service as men',[52] but rather:

> The case is this: The vast majority of the women citizens of this country, as of most countries, dislike this work, dislike it intensely, and would be grateful to the Government that would relieve them from it. We can afford to relieve them from it. There is not the necessity of putting this unpleasant duty on the women section of the country's citizenship.[53]

The government would relieve them of this burden.

Adding a dimension of paternalism to his pragmatism, O'Higgins also warned deputies that the matters juries dealt with were often unsuitable for women:

> I do not want to overstress it, but it is a fact that cases come before the courts not infrequently which one would not like to discuss

55 *DD*, vol. 18, 15 Feb. 1925, col. 468.   51 *DD*, vol. 18, 23 Feb. 1927, col. 754.   52 *DD*, vol. 18, 15 Feb. 1927, col. 468.   53 *DD*, vol. 18, 15 Feb. 1927, col. 489.

with the feminine members of one's own family. If you stand for the 1919 provision, compulsory jury service for all women, you have got to contemplate women members of your own family, or women members of a friend's family, being compelled to serve on juries when cases of that kind arise.[54]

More significant than the embarrassment it might have caused them, however, was the argument that women had more important duties to perform than wasting their time on jury service. Women, according to the minister of justice, had their own separate and distinct obligations, tending to the needs of their husbands and children, 'performing the normal function of womanhood in the State's economy'.[55] From the state's point of view, women were required in the home, not the jury box.

The minister for justice then turned his attention to those women's groups who opposed his legislation. Characterizing them as 'advanced propagandist women' who were 'self-appointed spokeswomen', the minister dismissed them as not representative, not able to speak for other women[56] – indeed, not 'normal'.[57] These groups, O'Higgins claimed, were trying to force the government into 'dragooning unwilling women' into jury service because they saw this bill as a 'slight on their sex'.[58] It was not, said the minister for justice. It was rather relieving women of an unwanted and unnecessary obligation. The government's position was that it was proper to confer on women citizens 'all the privileges of citizenship and such of the duties of citizenship as we thought it reasonable to impose upon them'.[59] Not that the government in general or the minister for justice in particular expected any gratitude for removing this burden from women. The minister for justice lamented:

> We find ourselves frequently in the position of preventing people getting something which they pretend they want, and which would not be good for them. Politically and economically, that seems to be our chronic position. In this matter I am really the champion

54 *DD*, vol. 18, col. 469, 15 Feb. 1927. For this same reason, O'Higgins also decided that there would be no women stenographers in the central criminal court and in the circuit courts throughout the country.   55 *SD*, vol. 8, 30 Mar. 1927, col. 697.   56 *DD*, vol. 18, 15 Feb. 1927, col. 468.   57 *DD*, vol. 18, 23 Feb. 1927, col. 757.   58 *DD*, vol. 18, 15 Feb. 1927, col. 467; *SD*, vol. 8, 30 Mar. 1927, col. 664.   59 *SD*, vol. 8, 30 Mar. 1927, col. 662.

of women in the State, but I never expect to get any gratitude for that.[60]

And he did not. Women's groups disagreed with O'Higgins and the government most vehemently. In fact, the 1927 juries bill generated a much broader, more organized and more sustained protest by various women's groups than the 1924 bill had. They were galvanized into action because, while the 1924 bill allowed women to opt out, the 1927 bill required them to opt in. Individual organizations joined forces to build a broad coalition to protest what they saw as an infringement of their rights. Prominent in the jury protest were the National Council of Women of Ireland, the Irish Women Workers' Union, the Women's Cooperative Guild, the Irish Women's Citizens Association, the Irish Women's Equality League and the Women's International Peace and Freedom League.

Their outrage found expression in political activities. They came together at the Joint Conference of Women's Societies to protest, plan strategy and publicize their opposition. They wrote letters to the newspapers. They canvassed every member of the Dáil. Some sent a deputation to Mr O'Higgins. Some sent a group of representatives to Lord Glenavy, the chair of the Seanad.

To feminists, the government's proposal to eliminate them from jury service was an attack on the principle of equality, was indeed an attack on democracy. To them the progression was clear: in 1924, the government exempted women on demand and thus, they believed, thwarted women's political and civic growth; in 1925, the government restricted certain positions in the civil service according to sex;[61] and now in 1927, this same government was attempting to remove them completely from jury service. They believed that the government was intent on taking away their rights, engaging in a 'steady, if stealthy, campaign against all those rights which women have so hardly won'.[62] They were outraged, and they were worried.

In response, feminists levelled a wide-ranging attack. Overall, they based their arguments on two broad principles: 1) that women had an inalienable right to citizenship as guaranteed in the constitution; and 2) that women had a unique contribution to make to the legal system, so the system itself would benefit if women participated in the jury system.

60 *SD*, vol. 8, 30 Mar. 1927, col. 691.   **61** See ch. 3.   **62** Letter to the editor, *Irish Times*, 17 Feb. 1927.

Feminists began their assault on the government's proposal by arguing that denying women their right to serve on juries was an assault on
democracy and 'a reflection of disability on women'.[63] Historically, other
groups who had been awarded the vote and could meet the property
qualifications automatically took their place in the jury box. It seemed
that women, however, were to be the exception.

Not only was the government's legislation an attack on democratic
principles, feminists contended, it was also unconstitutional. They
charged the government with violating its own constitution, which,
they believed, established the principle of complete equality between
men and women. Indeed, feminists pointed directly to article 3,
which, as noted earlier, stated that 'Every person without distinction
of sex, domiciled in the area of the ... Irish Free State ... is a citizen of the Irish Free State ...' It seemed clear to them that access to
jury service was a 'constitutional right which no Minister can tamper
with without violating Article 3 of the Constitution of the Irish Free
State'.[64]

Because men and women were equal under the law, feminists argued
that women should have the same rights and obligations as men, including such duties as jury service:

> Women must take part in the public life and accept the unpleas-
> ant duties as well as the pleasant ones. ... [I]t should be the duty
> of every woman to do all that is necessary in the public life of the
> country.[65]

They were not asking to be relieved of their duties. They did not want to
shirk their responsibilities.

Feminists also challenged the government's assumption that it had
the right to relieve women of their obligation and censured it for what
they saw as the arbitrary use of power. 'Is it not equally clear that, if the
duties can be arbitrarily curtailed, the rights and privileges can suffer the
same fate?' they asked.[66] What would be next? Would the administrative
cost of women voting be deemed too high and their franchise withdrawn?
As one woman said to the minister for justice, 'The next thing we hear

---

63 Letter of protest of the IWWU, Dublin, *Irish Times*, 28 Feb., 1927.   64 *Irish Times*,
22 Feb. 1927.   65 *Irish Times*, 11 Feb. 1927.   66 Letter to the editor, *Irish Independent*,
14 Feb. 1927.

may be a decision to abolish Parliamentary elections, owing to the small proportion of electors who vote.'[67] Where would it end?

Feminists also did not find particularly compelling the government's contention that women did not like jury service and hence should not serve. 'Where', they retorted, '[is] disinclination ... accepted as a valid reason for evasion of duty?'[68] 'How many men', women asked pointedly, 'were the same privilege [of exemption] theirs, would be found in the jury box?'[69] In their view, the issue was not whether men or women liked jury duty. Rather the issue was whether both men and women had an obligation to fulfil such service. As one woman noted:

> It is admitted that nobody, man or woman, likes the idea of jury service; but it seems to me only reasonable that nowadays, when women are sharing with men most of life's responsibilities, that it is rather childish to try to cut them off from one of the primary duties of citizenship on a plea that their feelings need special consideration.[70]

Moreover, women's reluctance to serve on juries did not mean that they were willing to give up the right to do so, did not mean that they believed the government should limit their citizenship. That was another matter entirely. One woman member of the Rathmines Urban Council explained that

> she was very glad that she had not to serve on juries, and she was not a bit keen on women acting as jurors. At the same time, she did not see why they should be excluded. A woman on trial might like to have some of her own sex on the jury. ... It seems a pity, after such a lot of expense, to withdraw this right from women without giving it a fair chance by a longer trial.[71]

Thus women's groups rejected the paternalistic pronouncements of the government about relieving them of an unpleasant task, emphasizing

---

67 Correspondence between Kevin O'Higgins and S.C. Harrison, *Irish Times*, 22 Feb. 1927. **68** Letter to President Cosgrave from the Hon. A. Spring Rice, president, Irish Women's Citizens and Local Government Association, 23 Feb. 1927, SPOD, S5317. **69** Letter to the editor, *Irish Times*, 15 Feb. 1927. **70** Letter to the editor, *Irish Times*, 17 Feb. 1927. **71** *Irish Times*, 11 Feb. 1927.

rather that this was an obligation of citizenship from which they should not be excluded.

Doubting that the government had women's best interest at heart, feminists pointedly questioned the government about its motives: 'The anxiety to spare citizens this disagreeable duty must have its roots in something other than benevolence, or why does it apply to women only?'[72] Feminists also did not find the government's rationale of fiscal economy particularly convincing. At issue, they argued, were principles of justice and women's constitutional rights. These principles could not and should not be measured in financial terms. 'Trifling expenses cannot honestly be set against the principle of common justice and public duty,' proclaimed the Irish Women's Citizens Association to the president of the Irish Free State.[73] Moreover, since women paid taxes equally with men, they 'cannot justly be deprived of a civic right on the score of economy or inconvenience'.[74]

Supporters of jury service for women also disagreed with the government's argument that the low number of women who served on juries reflected women's unwillingness to serve and hence justified the bill. They indicted O'Higgins for telling half-truths. They reiterated Hanna Sheehy Skeffington's point that the minister had neglected to mention that women were consistently told to 'stand aside' when they appeared for jury duty. This point particularly rankled supporters of jury service for women because they knew 'that for over three years women have been systematically excluded from juries because the State exerted its unlimited right to challenge against them'.[75] To fairly gauge the extent of women's service on juries, therefore, the question should be not how many women served, but how many women showed up for jury service. Again, Hanna Sheehy Skeffington directly challenged O'Higgins on this issue:

> Mr O'Higgins was asked during the debate (and by a deputation of women who interviewed him) to produce figures showing how many women answered their names when called for service.

72 Letter to the editor, *Irish Independent*, 1 Apr. 1927.   73 Letter to President Cosgrave from the Hon. A. Spring Rice, President, Irish Women's Citizens and Local Government Association, 23 Feb. 1927, S5317, SPOD.   74 Correspondence between Kevin O'Higgins and S.C. Harrison, *Irish Times*, 22 Feb. 1927.   75 Letter to the editor, *Irish Independent*, 22 Feb. 1927.

He replied that no such figures were available, knowing full well already that it is the court practice not to allow women to serve, because to use his own words, 'women in certain cases are loathe to convict!' There is no record available, in fact, no note being taken of the number of women challenged by either State or prisoners, and Mr O'Higgins' statement, therefore, is based on a deliberate misrepresentation.[76]

Women, moreover, were treated shabbily when they did appear for jury service, 'often kept days – in some cases actually weeks – coming to Court, to be finally challenged and told to "stand by"'.[77] Ultimately, they might be told simply that 'no women jurors were required'.[78] Indeed, given such practices, what was surprising was not the low numbers of women who served on juries but rather the fact that women actually continued to appear for jury service at all.

Feminists further criticized O'Higgins for characterizing them as 'self-appointed spokeswomen' who supposedly did not speak for their sex.[79] 'Who', women asked, 'gave him a mandate on the subject? Why drag in this "fancy legislation" in a dying Parliament and rush it through?'[80] The government, they noted, had not consulted women on this issue but rather had acted in isolation, 'legislating for us in the dark – wasting their precious time, public money, and golden opportunities'.[81] Who then could be characterized as the self-appointed spokesperson? Why did the male government know better than women what women wanted? The government had simply proclaimed that women did not want to sit on juries 'without any public steps being taken to consult women, or even to seek the advice of their representative societies'.[82]

Women's groups pointed out to the government that, far from being an isolated minority, they had a wide following among a broad spectrum of women in a coalition that crossed classes, religions and political parties. They noted that their protest found support among 'women members of county and urban councils, women vice-chairmen [*sic*] of public boards,

76 Letter to the editor, *Voice of Labour*, 12 Mar. 1927.   **77** Letter to the editor, *Irish Times*, 18 Feb. 1927.   **78** Letter to the editor, *Voice of Labour*, 12 Mar. 1927.   **79** *SD*, 30 Mar. 1927, vol. 8, col. 664; *DD*, 15 Feb. 1927, vol. 18, col. 468.   **80** Letter to the editor, *Irish Times*, 18 Feb. 1927.   **81** Letter to the editor, *Irish Independent*, 14 Feb. 1927.   **82** Correspondence between Kevin O'Higgins and S.C. Harrison, *Irish Times*, 22 Feb. 1927.

women Senators, graduates, women lawyers, doctors, teachers, journal-
ists and prominent business women ... women in every political party
– Labour, Republican, Government and Unionist'.[83] The implication was
clear: the government would do well to have the same kind of support

Moreover, in women's eyes, the government had not given jury service for women a fair chance. Their right to serve on juries had only
been in operation since 1918 – less than ten years. This was, in their
view, scarcely sufficient time to allow women and men to adjust to wom-
en's new public role in the jury box. Women needed more time to feel
comfortable in courtrooms and jury boxes, in areas which had previously been closed to them. Similarly, those involved in the legal process
needed time to accept women as jurors. The concept of the woman juror
needed to be supported, not thwarted, by the state. And, society needed
time to accept this broadened definition of what was appropriate for
women to do.

The consequences of not giving women that time, of removing women
from jury service would be far-reaching, feminists argued. It would
restrict women's horizons, inhibit their interest in public affairs and
hinder their development as public persons, 'closing the door to a wide
field of opportunity and service to women for generations to come'.[84] It
would, in fact, deny women a public identity within the state. As Jennie
Wyse Power, now a senator of the Irish Free State, declared:

> [I]f this Bill becomes law, the civic spirit that is developing in
> women will be arrested. In fact, the suggestions that there shall be
> only male jurors in the future cuts at the very root of this develop-
> ment of the awakening of the civic spirit. We all know that in the
> past this spirit had been repressed and became stunted and did
> not grow. But by the happenings, political happenings if you like,
> during the last 50 years the men who led political movements and
> carried them in the main to success, utilised women in order to
> achieve their object. That utilization of women helped in a great
> degree their civic spirit.[85]

Now, after independence, those who came to power as a result of those
'political happenings' were trying to exclude women from the civic life of

83 Letter to the editor, *Irish Independent*, 22 Feb. 1927.   84 Letter to the editor, *Irish Independent*, 14 Feb. 1927.   85 *SD*, vol. 8, 30 Mar. 1927, cols 682–3.

the nascent state. Those women who had supported the government felt betrayed. Writing to the minister for justice, one woman stated, 'I cannot but regret deeply that you, sir, on behalf of the first free Government in Ireland, should have consented to put your hand to this bill.'[86] The door that the struggle for independence had flung open was now being closed tighter and tighter.

It was, moreover, more than a question of rights and responsibilities. Many of the women's groups accepted and believed in the complementary nature of the sexes. They argued that women jurors would confer benefits on the system that men could not. Using society's view that women's 'natural role' was motherhood, feminists argued that women, therefore, had something unique, something different from men to contribute. These women asserted that, because of their role as child-bearers, -rearers and -nurturers, women had insights denied men. These insights made their presence on juries mandatory. To say otherwise, as the government was doing, to say that women could be excluded from juries and nothing would be lost, 'that women's contributions would not be significant enough to warrant the difficulties they and their presence created',[87] was patently false. Thus, women's groups used society's argument about natural roles to further their own ends, to assert their unique public value in a patriarchal society that devalued their political personas.

Because men and women were different, women's groups maintained, the interests of justice demanded that there be mixed juries:

> Juries exist that justice may be done and 'feminists' hold that this is more likely to be achieved when the mental qualities of both sexes are brought to bear on the evidence.[88]

Or as the Irish Women Workers' Union protested:

> [A]s men and women are alike liable to stand in the dock as offenders against the law, it is just and right that the question of their guilt should be submitted to juries consisting of both men and women; and that, as in the case of families, judicious treatment of

86 Correspondence between O'Higgins and S.C. Harrison, *Irish Times*, 22 Feb. 1927.   87 *DD*, vol. 18, 15 Feb. 1927, cols 487–9.   88 Letter to the editor, *Irish Times*, 15 Feb. 1927.

sons and daughters demands the combined wisdom of the mother and father, so, in the case of offenders against the law, justice and mercy can be assured only through the combined wisdom of men and women jurors.[89]

For similar reasons, women's groups stressed that women's presence on juries was vital in cases concerning other women and children, 'for whose suffering and whose needs women have a special understanding'.[90] The Irish Save the Children Fund, for example, believed that 'the presence of women on juries in all cases affecting children is absolutely essential'.[91] As one woman asked:

> Would any mother be capable of wishing her child to appear in a court of law composed exclusively of men? Surely, ordinary common decency of feelings demands that there should be women on the juries which try these cases.[92]

Nor was it only children who needed women in the jury box. Other women involved in the judicial process did also. Thus, it was

> the opinion of the representative women's societies, who have been seriously considering the question, that where a woman is prisoner, plaintiff, defendant or principal witness, a mixed jury should be formed. It has always been recognised that a prisoner is entitled to be tried by his or her peers, and without a woman on the jury a woman cannot be tried in this way.[93]

In all cases involving women and children, therefore, women's groups argued, there should be women on the jury.

It did not matter if these were the 'unsavoury' cases. Feminists proclaimed that they were not 'such tender plants as the Victorians pretended, and, indeed, some men are far more shockable but are not excused from jury service for that'.[94] In most cases, they pointed out, women took part in those unsavoury cases and hence a mixed jury was

89 *Irish Times*, 28 Feb. 1927. **90** Letter to the editor, *Irish Times*, 15 Feb. 1927. **91** Letter to President Cosgrave from the Irish Save the Children Fund, 28 Feb. 1927, File S.5317, SPOD. **92** Letter to the editor, *Irish Times*, 17 Feb. 1927. **93** *Irish Times*, 17 Apr. 1927. **94** Letter to the editor, *Irish Times*, 15 Feb. 1927.

necessary: 'As unsavoury cases are not created by men alone, they should not be dealt with by men alone.'[95]

By pointing to the realities of women's lives, feminists exposed the myth of women as the fair sex which needed protection from the harshness of real life. Who protected working-class women from the harshness of labour? Who sheltered nurses and social workers from offensive encounters? Why was paternalistic protection only invoked when women tried to exercise their rights as citizens?

Although feminists did not directly confront society's belief that the 'natural' role of women was motherhood, they did challenge the absolute equation of womanhood with motherhood. They pointed out that women were mothers for only part of the time, that 'they did not have children clinging all their lives'.[96] Hence it was illogical to exclude all women for all time on the rationale that they had a more important service to perform to the state. The government's bill sought to exclude not simply mothers, but women as a class from jury duty.

Moreover, feminists repudiated the prevailing public/private dichotomy which sought to keep them from crossing from the home to the courtroom. They strongly disputed the notion that, if a woman were a wife and mother, she could not be an active public citizen. They rejected the assumption that care of husbands and families restricted women exclusively to the domestic sphere. It was an argument they had heard before in the campaign for suffrage. As one woman wrote:

> It is extraordinary how the poor, dinnerless husband manages to survive in this country as an argument against almost any kind of progress. In pre-war days it was the Parliamentary franchise. If a woman left her home for the period of time necessary to record her vote it might entail the dread possibility of her husband's having no dinner (masculine imagination apparently could picture no greater calamity).
>
> One is really ashamed of the type of argument which is being used to-day in the Free State in order to push women back into the dark ages. Surely the argument of the neglected home and husband

---

95 'Reply of the Women's Citizens Association to the reasons advanced by the minister of justice for the exclusion of women from jury service under the juries bill', SPOD, S5317. **97** Letter to the editor, *Irish Independent*, 1 Apr. 1927.

has become too thin and poor to be referred to save by way of joke in any civilised country.[97]

'The poor dinnerless husband' excuse was not restricted to Ireland but was part of a general, pervasive patriarchal ideology. Years later, in a case in the US (Hoyt v. Florida, 1961) about the issue of jury service for women, this sentiment was expressed by one of the lawyers who opposed women serving on juries: 'Well, Mr Chief Justice ... they have to cook the dinner.'[98] According to the American historian, Linda Kerber, the import of this sentiment was that it 'highlighted the bond between those whose dinners were cooked and those who were freed from their civic obligation of jury service so that they could cook those dinners'.[99] I would argue that it could very easily also apply to Ireland.

Feminists argued that women left their homes for long periods of time for all sorts of reasons – for work, for leisure activities, for entertainment. Why, then, could they not leave their homes to participate in public affairs? they asked. Jury duty was not a full-time occupation, but rather a sporadic and short interruption of one's daily life.

As evidence of the importance and suitability of women serving on juries, feminists pointed to the experience of women jurors in England and in some states in the United States. For example, one letter cited statements from three US judges commending women for their service on juries.[100] Another quoted an English lawyer who spoke of the advantages of having women on juries.[101] The women of the Irish Free State, they believed, were 'as willing as anxious and as capable of fulfilling this civic duty as the women of other countries'.[102]

These arguments appear, to some extent, to have pricked the conscience of a number of legislators. Some senators and deputies felt the government's original bill was too draconian and sought a compromise. The government, therefore, accepted an amendment to its legislation that, although exempting women as a class from jury service, allowed

97 Letter to the editor, *Irish Times*, 17 Feb. 1927. **98** Kerber, Linda, 'Women and the obligations of citizenship' in Linda Kerber, Alice Kessler-Harris & Kathryn Kish Sklar, *US history as women's history: new feminist essays* (Chapel Hill, 1995). The case was Hoyt v. Florida, 368 US. 57, decided by the Supreme Court of the United States in 1961. **99** Ibid. **100** Letter to the editor, *Irish Times*, 18 Feb. 1927. **101** Letter to the editor, *Irish Times*, 15 Feb. 1927. **102** 'Reply of the Women's Citizens Association to the Minister for Justice', SPOD, S 5317.

individuals to serve if they so decided. Under this revised provision, women could opt in and volunteer to serve on juries. It was, however, merely the illusion of choice. Seemingly, the amendment left women free to enter the public sphere; but, in reality, the proviso ensured that few, if any, would actually do so. The amendment was a political strategy that allowed deputies and senators to ease their consciences. The end result, however, would be much the same as the government's original legislation intended: no women jurors.

Not surprisingly, the amendment was introduced without consultation with the various women's groups, who understood what its effect would be and opposed it. Requiring volunteers, they said, would place an 'unfair burden upon the conscientious woman'.[103] 'Jury service is not philanthropy', they argued, and the formation of mixed juries 'should not be left to the chance of an adequate supply of volunteers'.[104] Just as the average man was compelled to serve, so also should the average woman be.[105]

Moreover, making jury service voluntary would insure that only a very few women would actually serve. Women could be told to 'stand aside' with even more impunity. Women defendants, plaintiffs and witnesses would continue to be deprived of the presence of women in the jury box. Under this amendment, therefore, mixed juries would not be secured, and the interests of justice would not be met.

Volunteer jury service would also place an incredible strain upon those who had the courage to volunteer, making it almost impossible for them to seek an exemption if the need should arise. According to Senator Jennie Wyse Power:

> [T]he woman who comes forward and places her name upon the voluntary panel if the time comes when she has ever to seek exemption her position will be a most difficult one indeed. Jibes and sneers are very often flung about upon this question and if a woman, I repeat, who had the courage or the strength to put her name down for the voluntary panel, should come and claim exemption on proper and right grounds we can all realise the taunts that may be flung at her and her sex.[106]

---

103 *Irish Times*, 4 Mar. 1927.   104 Pamphlet, SPOD, S.5317.   105 Pamphlet, SPOD, S.5317.   106 *SD*, vol. 8, 8 Apr. 1927, col. 803.

This was an obvious deterrent to women who might otherwise have chosen to put their names forward.

Women's organizations saw the amendment as an attempt to divide women, to classify them into acceptable and non-acceptable, normal and abnormal. They asserted that those women who were prepared to serve on juries had already been deliberately categorized as 'abnormal' and that 'the implication that only abnormal women were prepared to serve upon a jury, was a stigma upon [all] women'.[107] The Joint Conference of Women's Societies declared that the voluntary panel 'lays a stigma upon all women to imply that only the abnormal are prepared to serve on juries'.[108]

Their suspicions were well founded. Indeed those women who fought the government on this issue were ridiculed and castigated in the Dáil, in the Seanad and in the press. Those opposing jury service for women argued that the respectable elements of society would never wish to enter a jury box. They articulated a gender ideology that located women solely in the home. For example, a number of the newspapers of the day asserted that 'real women' or 'ladies' had no desire to serve on juries, to be wrenched from 'the bosoms of their families, from their cherished household duties, from the preparation of their husbands' dinners'.[109] Indeed one editorial stated this quite clearly:

> The suffragist possibly voices the opinion of her kind, but we doubt if she speaks for 1/2 to 1 per cent of the women of Ireland in this matter. ... let any woman who wants to serve lodge her claim. ... That will preserve the cherished right to say guilty or not guilty according to her judgment ... And it will leave the real woman free to attend to her household and her family instead of keeping her husband at home to mind the baby and boil the potatoes while she is away at court trying to do a man's work.[110]

If neither 'ladies' nor 'real women' wished to serve on juries, who were those who did wish to exercise this right? In the Dáil, Kevin O'Higgins answered that question by claiming that women who wished to serve on

---

107 *Irish Times*, 4 Mar. 1927. 108 Joint Conference of Women's Societies, SPOD, S.5317. 109 Editorial, *Dundalk Democrat*, quoted in the *Irish Independent*, 14 Feb. 1927. See also, for example, articles in the *Irish Independent*, *Dundalk Democrat* and *Evening Herald*. 110 Editorial, *Irish Independent*, 14 Feb. 1927.

juries were the 'advanced propagandist women', the minority who were clearly not the norm:

> Many of these women are themselves outstanding examples of the capacity of women to take their place in public life and to render useful service. But are they normal or the exception? I submit to Deputies that they are the exception rather than the normal, and that they are well aware themselves that they are the exception rather than the normal.[111]

In the Seanad, one member characterized the pro-jury women as 'certain women of advanced or perhaps intellectual views' who were 'whipping up' the mass of women in the country who really were not anxious to serve on juries.[112]

The press added its own ridicule, describing women's groups as the 'eternal spouters', atypical and offensive:

> The women of the Free State are not to be judged by their loud-voiced, self-constituted advocates, who are eternally spouting and writing to the newspapers and marching in processions.[113]

To the press, these women constituted nothing more than 'a few ladies who have nothing else to do but gad about, and who dearly love the limelight'.[114] Some of them indeed, the press claimed, were nothing more than 'feminists' who 'wanted women to imitate men'.[115]

In perhaps the most damaging charge made against the women who wanted to participate in the political life of the state, they were dismissed as unfulfilled and envious, women who supposedly had not fulfilled their 'natural' role as mother and wife and allegedly were jealous of those who had. One deputy stated this very clearly in the Dáil:

> [B]etween the ages of twenty and forty the majority of women ... [have] a much more important duty to perform to the State than service on juries, that their functions were motherhood and looking

111 *DD*, vol. 18, 23 Feb. 1927, col. 757. 112 *SD*, vol. 8, 8 Apr. 1927, col. 787. 113 Editorial, *Kilkenny People*, quoted in the *Irish Independent*, 1 Mar. 1927. 114 Editorial, *Dundalk Democrat*, quoted in the *Irish Independent*, 14 Feb. 1927. 115 Editorial, *Irish Independent*, 11 Feb. 1927.

after their families, and they objected to these other women, *who have missed these functions* [emphasis added], and who wanted to drive to serve on juries those who have something else to do.[116]

By such attacks on the women who wished to participate in the political life of the state, those opposed to such a role for women sought to deride and divide women and intimidate some who might have thought of identifying with or joining these various women's groups. They also attempted to devalue and trivialize women's arguments.

Despite these attacks, in the battle over the 1927 juries bill, women's groups exercised their political rights with skill and determination. In the end, however, the amended bill became law. The reasons for their lack of success and the significance that jury service assumed lay embedded in the climate of post-independence Ireland.

The question of jury service for women was significant because as early as 1924 it set up the parameters for the debate over women's role in the state. Feminists were on notice that the government's intention was to create a gendered definition of citizenship that would, ultimately, leave them as second-class citizens.

The issue of jury service clearly revealed the depth of the reaction against women participating in public life. The praise and gratitude women had received for their part in the Anglo-Irish War had changed to a condemnation of them and their role in the Civil War. Compare, for example, the statement by Michael Collins of July 1922 concerning women's role in the Anglo-Irish War – 'Few appreciate what Ireland owes to the women who stood their ground during the first few years and no thanks that anyone can bestow on them will be too great'[117] – to that of the pro-Treaty historian P.S. O'Hegarty, who wrote that during the Civil War, Dublin was full of 'hysterical women', who had been turned into 'unlovely, destructive-minded, arid begetters of violence' by the revolution.[118] In a very telling passage, O'Hegarty wrote:

---

116 *DD*, vol. 18, 22 Mar. 1927, col. 26.   117 Quoted in Conlon, *Cumann na mBan*, pp 263–4.   118 O'Hegarty, *The victory of Sinn Féin*, p. 58. It is interesting to note that O'Hegarty misrepresents the position of Inghinidhe na hÉireann in this work, claiming that, unlike the women of 1922, they restricted their work to 'women's work'. Of course, Inghinidhe na hÉireann was a much more militant organization, which saw itself as capable of fighting for Ireland's freedom.

Left to himself, man is comparatively harmless. He will always exchange smokes and drinks and jokes with his enemy, and he will always pity the 'poor devil' and wish that the whole business was over ... It is woman ... with her implacability, her bitterness, her hysteria, that makes a devil of him. The Suffragettes used to tell us that with women in political power there would be no more war. We know that with women in political power there would be no more peace.[119]

The hostility to the Treaty of the overwhelming majority of the members of Cumann na mBan, as well as that of the women deputies in the Dáil, redounded against women. In a sense, they were blamed for the Civil War. O'Hegarty, for example, blamed women for the divisiveness and violence which plagued the country – a position clearly not supported by the events of the period.[120] However, the Civil War was such a devastating experience that the need to scapegoat, to blame was enormous. Women were one easy and obvious target.

This condemnation of women led, in turn, to a more general questioning of whether women belonged in public life at all. Indeed, the government was confronted by the fact that some of its most implacable opponents were women. Furthermore, even within the government's own party, women like Jennie Wyse Power were prominent in the dissident wing, which had severely criticized the government. Indeed Jennie Wyse Power had directly challenged the government in the Seanad on the issue of jury service. By eliminating women from public life, the government may have thought it was eradicating a source of criticism, a font of disapproval.

There were, however, other less pragmatic reasons for the gendered definition of citizenship. There seemed to be, in fact, a conceptual and experiential gap between the current leaders of the Free State, such as Kevin O'Higgins, and the nationalist feminist women who led the debate on the juries issue. A new state, these women concluded, demanded a new and revised gender ideology. Drawing on the tradition of Inghinidhe na hÉireann, on 1916, women saw themselves as equal before the law, as equal citizens with the same rights and responsibilities. They believed

119 O'Hegarty, *The victory of Sinn Féin*, p. 105.   120 For a detailed discussion of the negotiations that occurred in the months prior to the Civil War, see my book *Portrait of a revolutionary*.

that women would assume their proper role as full citizens and hence contribute their unique insights to the public realm.

However, the government at the time did not follow in the footsteps of Connolly and Pearse, men who not only believed in women's rights but also had practical experience working with the women of Inghinidhe na hÉireann and the Citizen Army. Kevin O'Higgins, for example, had neither. His view of women seemed to be quite traditional; his early biographer described it as 'almost medieval'.[121]

Nor, to use Kevin O'Higgins again as an example, was there the intellectual commitment to women's equality, to women's worth in the public sphere, which feminist nationalist women had anticipated. What was being articulated was unbridled patriarchy. During the debates in the Dáil and Seanad, O'Higgins's view was simply that women were unnecessary to the working of the legal system and hence should be eliminated. What was missing was the commitment to equality which would actively seek to bring women into the system. What was also missing was the belief that women had something to contribute to the system, that, in fact, the legal system would benefit from having women jurors, despite whatever the extra expense and administrative burden of the women juror. Thus during the debates on this issue, feminists and their government opponents were talking across a conceptual and experiential gulf that made any type of agreement virtually impossible.

The government's restrictive legislation can also be interpreted as an attempt to restore traditional order and hierarchy after the chaos of the Anglo-Irish War and Civil War and an attempt to stem the 'moral deterioration' that seemed to be creeping through the country in the 1920s. Changing gender relations seemed to be indicative of this deterioration.

---

121 Terence de Vere White, *Kevin O'Higgins* (Dublin, 1948), p. 169. Kevin O'Higgins joined the independence movement through the Volunteers after the outbreak of the First World War. Like many of the Volunteers, his intention to participate in the 1916 Rising was thwarted by the confusion of the time. His main contribution was in the department of local government under William T. Cosgrave. In this capacity, he may have been involved with nationalist women who served as judges, but his biographer makes no mention of this. O'Higgins' views on women were probably also influenced by the fact that he had studied to be a priest and seemed to take his religion quite seriously. His earlier biographer noted that he fasted for half a year before he married, a concept de Vere White likened to the 'idealized conception of a dedicated knight'. I, however, believe all of this to be apocryphal.

In some eyes, women were forgetting that indeed their natural and correct role was in the home. They were venturing out – into the public sphere to serve on juries, to infiltrate the professions, to compete for jobs. For many, jury service was thus symptomatic and symbolic: symptomatic of the aggressive spirit propelling women to leave their natural habitat; symbolic of the desire of women to infiltrate a man's world, to bob their hair, to smoke and drink in public and demonstrate disdain for the traditional conventions that kept them under control – to become the 'fag-smoking, jazz-dancing, lip-sticking flappers' against which the *Kilkenny People*, for example, raged.[122] Thus, by keeping women off of jury service, the government and its allies tried to strengthen and reaffirm the message that only abnormal women attempted to enter the male domain, that women belonged in the home, tending to the needs of their husbands and children. In this definition of a post-revolutionary identity, women's role would be restricted to the hearth and home wherein they could keep alive the traditional cultural values. It bespoke an unfinished revolution.

Finally, it is possible that the Free State used women as means of both demonstrating and consolidating its power. The government compensated for its inability to control much of what was happening around it by asserting its power over women. In this, the government's response would be typical of post-revolutionary societies, which often consolidate their power by enacting measures against women, such as forbidding women's political participation, outlawing abortion, prohibiting wage-earning by mothers, imposing female dress codes.[123] In these concerns, the government had the backing of the Catholic church.

Whatever motivated the government, it was clear, as the jury issue demonstrated, that feminists were not going to accept the government's

---

122 *Kilkenny People*, quoted in the *Irish Independent*, 1 Mar. 1927. 123 '[E]mergent rulers have legitimized domination, strength, central authority, and ruling power as masculine (enemies, outsiders, subversives, weakness as feminine) and made that code literal in laws (forbidding women's political participation, outlawing abortion, prohibiting wage-earning by mothers, imposing female dress codes) that put women in their place. These actions and their timing make little sense in themselves; in most instances, the state had nothing immediate or material to gain from the control of women. The actions can only be made sense of as part of an analysis of the construction and consolidation of power. An assertion of control or strength was given form as a policy about women.' Joan Wallach Scott, 'Gender: a useful category of historical analysis' in Joan Wallach Scott (ed.), *Gender and the politics of history* (New York, 1988), p. 47.

restrictions without an argument. Feminists understood that much more was at stake than simply the right to enter a jury box. The debate was about power – political power, public power. And, it was a share of power that feminists were demanding.

To achieve this, feminists began to construct an ideological model for women which was broader, more inclusive. They did not go as far as the editors of *Bean na hÉireann* and proclaim that domesticity was boring. Rather they took a more moderate position, arguing for a construction of womanhood that would allow for both a public identity and a private identity.

Through their protest, feminists asserted themselves as women citizens – a construct they invested with power and privilege, rights and responsibilities. They proclaimed that woman as citizen was not incompatible with woman as mother, as wife or as homemaker. They thus provided an alternative model of womanhood to the narrow view expressed by the government and the society by insisting that women had both a right and obligation to add their talents, their perspective, their insights to the development of the new state.

Moreover, these women subverted the dominant discourse to their own ends by accepting society's argument that women had some type of natural link to motherhood, but using that as a reason why women must, therefore, serve on juries, why their service was essential to the proper functioning of the legal system. Making common cause with first-wave feminists in countries such as the United States and England, these Irish women 'transformed a misogynistic discourse about differences between the sexes into an alternative discourse about female uniqueness designed to advance women's status and opportunities'.[124]

In the struggle over jury service, feminists articulated their demand for political equality and access to the public sphere of power. In this way, they challenged the patriarchal world view articulated by the government. The government, however, pressed on with restrictive gender legislation. Next under attack would be women's right to work.

124 Linda Gordon, 'On difference', *Genders*, 10 (Spring, 1991), p. 91.

3

For men only: the right to employment

Women's right to gainful employment, to work outside the home, was a contentious issue in the Irish Free State. This debate was obviously grounded in, and part of, the growing sentiment that women needed to be returned to that bastion of domesticity, the home, and also that women had to be reminded of their subordinate role in society. Jobs were for men; women need not apply.

The economic climate of the debate was obviously very important. The 1920s and 1930s were, of course, times of economic recession and growing joblessness. Throughout Europe, governments were bedevilled by unemployment. Ireland was no exception. In an effort to combat the problem, it set up a Committee on the Relief of Unemployment in 1927.

The Irish government was hampered in finding a solution by its own ideology. According to J.J. Lee, Cosgrave's 'cabinet … took the view that the poor were responsible for their poverty. They should pay for their lack of moral fibre.'[1] Diarmaid Ferriter concurs with Lee. Ferriter argues that some members of the government could not see the value of welfare measures, which Ferriter believed was the result of the 'Victorian climate in which many of them grew to adulthood'.[2] The most extreme example of this view was the oft-quoted statement by Patrick McGilligan, who in 1924 assumed the position of minister for industry and commerce. He stated that 'People may have to die in this country, and may have to die from starvation.' While he did not relish this idea, he believed that 'it is no function of government to provide work for anybody'.[3]

The Irish Women Workers' Union, obviously concerned about this issue, requested that the government appoint a woman to the Committee on the Relief of Unemployment. President Cosgrave refused.[4] His

---

1 Lee, *Ireland*, p. 124. 2 Ibid.; Diarmaid Ferriter, *The transformation of Ireland, 1900–2000* (London, 2004), p. 316. 3 Quoted in Lee, *Ireland*, p. 127. 4 Minutes of the executive committee, IWWU, minute book 5, 23 Nov. 1927, IWWU Archives. An additional request in 1928 that the government set up a committee of women to deal with unemployment among women did not seem to produce a result. Minutes of the executive committee, IWWU, minute book 5, 25 Apr. 1928, IWWU Archives.

refusal was a clear signal of the government's priorities and assessment of the dimension of the unemployment problem. Male politicians were worried about male employment. Not surprisingly, therefore, when the final report was issued, it contained no reference whatsoever to women.[5]

Arguments about women's employment had many layers. The right to work for married women, for example, was much debated. The general belief was that once married, a woman's obligation was to mind the hearth and home while her husband's responsibility was to provide financial support. Even the Irish Women Workers' Union had doubts about the right of its married members to employment outside the home – despite the fact that their income was often vital to sustaining their families. This issue was regularly debated at IWWU meetings.[6] The overriding notion was that men were, and, perhaps more significantly, had the right to be, the breadwinners, the sole financial support of their families.

The situation was not much better for single women. Their employment – both the type of jobs available to them and their promotion within those jobs – was also limited by the prevailing ideology, which viewed all women as wives (or potential wives) with husbands to support them. Jobs for these women were deemed temporary, until they married, and/ or unnecessary for the actual support of families – the ubiquitous and

5 Minutes of the executive committee, IWWU, minute book 5, 29 Feb. 1928, IWWU Archives. It would be inaccurate to think that the IWWU was concerned only with women's employment. In 1925, it sent a notice, 'Remember the Unemployed', to all members of the Dáil and Seanad, urging them to take on the issue of unemployment for both men and women. It said that 'it is the clear duty of a Government to save from destitution every work-willing citizen compulsorily unemployed. Upon you, members of the Oireachtas, falls the responsibility to see that the executive council provide MAINTENANCE for the men and women unable to find work. This can only be done BY WIDE AND IMMEDIATE EXTENSION OF UNEMPLOYMENT BENEFIT. The men, women, and children who are now hungry cannot wait till a general industrial development provides them with more work. But MORE WORK MUST BE FOUND, and found quickly. Here are immediate and practical ways in which the Government can help:- 1. By maintaining a HIGH STANDARD OF WAGES, and thus giving a stimulus to home markets by increasing the purchasing power of the people. 2. By specifying IRISH MANUFACTURES ARTICLES in all Government contracts and work carried our by Government grants. 3. By RAISING THE SCHOOL LEAVING AGE TO 16, and so preventing children of 14 and 15 from flooding the labour market and displacing adult workers. REMEMBER THE UNEMPLOYED.' *Irish Independent*, 3 Nov. 1925.   6 Mary E. Daly, 'Women, work and trade unionism' in Margaret MacCurtain & Donnchadh Ó Corráin (eds), *Women in Irish society* (Dublin, 1978), p. 75

damaging concept of 'pin money'. Women were, therefore, denied training, promotion and comparable rates of pay.

The fact that these assumptions did not reflect the reality of life for a
large number of women did not alter the terms of the debate. Reality was
not central in influencing the government's position. It was conveniently
overlooked.

Moreover, throughout post-war Europe, there was resentment over
women working outside the home. The perception was that women had
taken over men's jobs – especially during the First World War – and
were reluctant to give them back, to move out of jobs that were, on the
whole, more interesting and better paid. A letter to the editor in the *Irish
Independent* by a man who protested against 'feminism run riot' was
typical: 'The present unemployment is not altogether due to industrial
depression, but to the fact that women got the men's jobs during the war,
and have kept them.'[7]

In Ireland, the perception was that the number of women at work was
increasing at the expense of men. This was not borne out by the facts. In
reality, Irish women's employment in the 1920s was still overwhelming
in two sectors of the economy – farming and domestic service. In 1926,
60 per cent of women workers were employed in these two occupations.[8]
Women's employment did show a slight increase in other areas. In 1936,
for example, 'women accounted for 31.3 percent of the manufacturing
workforce compared with 26.6 percent ten years earlier'.[9] These jobs,
however, tended to be in new industries, and women were concentrated
in unskilled or semi-skilled jobs. It was not a substitution of female for
male workers.[10]

It was also not simply about numbers. The prevailing gender ideology
also shaped and constructed attitudes towards employment. These attitudes denied women the right to equal employment opportunities, and in
fact denied the very idea of a meritocracy for men and women. Indeed,
the belief that women had a right to work outside the home was not
acknowledged in the dominant discourse. Instead, women's employment
became intertwined with the need to re-establish order and hierarchy,
to reassert masculine privilege and control. In the post-revolutionary

7 Letter to the editor, *Irish Independent*, 30 May 1925. 8 Daly, 'Women, work and
trade unionism', p. 72. 9 Mary E. Daly, *Industrial development and Irish national identity, 1922–1939* (Syracuse, 1992), pp 124–5. 10 Ibid.

period, a man's right to work and to support women and children was tied directly to definitions of masculinity, to who held power and who wielded control. Keeping women out of the workforce enforced their dependency on men and strengthened patriarchal dominance.

Concern about gender – about gender roles and gender hierarchy – permeated the employment issue. As one deputy noted: '[W]omen occupy a position of equality today with men that never would have been contemplated years ago.'[11] Women, it was popularly believed, had moved into every arena, and simply no longer knew or stayed in their place. They were everywhere: in the professions, in the trades, in the offices. As one speaker noted in the Dáil:

> I am an old-fashioned person and frankly not enthusiastic about the modern change in the relation of the sexes. It is the most revolutionary thing that has happened in our time. I believe that 200 or 300 years hence, when a historian writes the history of the last fifty years, he [*sic*] will not speak of the wireless or the development of the motor car or of the Shannon scheme as the most striking fact of the last twenty-five years of the nineteenth century and the first twenty-five years of the twentieth century. He will say the change in the position of women is the most significant and striking fact. It was in that epoch that woman left her home to take up a career and, in consequence, you now have woman in almost every sphere of life except the Church and the Army ...[12]

Clearly, women's employment offered the possibility of independence, of freedom from male domination – be it the dominance of husbands or fathers or brothers. The spectre of the 1920s flapper – economically independent and free from paternalistic control – seemed a portent of things to come if women's employment were left unchecked.

However, that was not the story in Ireland, where the right to work for single women was not progressing. As the economic historian Mary E. Daly points out:

> The fact that a high proportion of single women were not in paid employment held considerable implications for their welfare, status, and security; it assumes even greater significance in the light of their

11 *DD*, 18 Nov. 1925, vol. 13, col. 519.   12 Ibid., col. 512.

poor marriage prospects. By 1926, 24 per cent of women in the age-group 45 to 54 were single and were likely to remain so for life.[13]

It is within this context that women's right to work outside the home came under increasing attack. In 1925, the Cosgrave government limited the right of women to sit for examinations in the civil service. In the 1930s, a marriage bar was formally introduced for women teachers and eventually applied to the entire civil service. In 1935, the de Valera government sponsored legislation – the conditions of employment bill, 1936 – which gave the minister for industry and commerce the right to limit the number of women employed in any given industry.

Collectively, this legislation clearly and forthrightly announced that in the Irish Free State the priority was men's employment and women – regardless of whether they were self-supporting or not – had their employment prospects severely limited. The employment legislation further eroded women's status and strengthened the patriarchal nature of the Irish Free State.

Certainly, the question of gender hierarchy was central to the 1925 debate on women's employment in the civil service. It was a gender hierarchy that privileged married men above all, then single men; after these classes of men came women – married and single, alternating depending on the issue. In keeping with this ideology, in December 1924 the government announced that examination for junior administrative positions would be restricted to men only. A prospective woman candidate threatened to take legal action, claiming that the government did not have the power to exclude on the basis of sex. The attorney general concurred. He concluded that, according to the Civil Service Regulation Act of 1924, competitive examinations were to be open to all citizens of the Free State who 'pay the fees and possess the qualifications as to age, health, and character prescribed by the regulations'. While there were exemptions to this principle, the attorney general concluded that sex was not a relevant category for exclusion. He, therefore, concluded 'that the Commissioners had no power to make the regulations excluding women from this examination'.[14]

---

13 Mary E. Daly, 'Women in the Irish Free State, 1922–39: the interaction between economics and ideology', *Journal of Women's History*, 6:4 & 7:1 (Winter/Spring, 1995), pp 102–3.   14 Memo to the department of finance from the attorney general, 15 Dec. 1924, S.4195, NA.

In light of the attorney general's decision, the government was forced to seek the necessary authority from the Dáil 'to confine examinations to person of one sex'.[15] The subsequent debate revealed the tensions and gender anxieties besetting the Free State. Indeed, the government's position, as outlined by the minister for finance, Ernest Blythe, clearly articulated the prevailing belief that the traditional gender hierarchy was under attack and needed to be bolstered, needed to be set right. Once that was accomplished, employment – in particular employment in the civil service – would flow according to 'normal' patterns.

The minister, therefore, introduced the bill as simply a mechanism to ensure that the civil service would function smoothly and efficiently, in accordance with the prescribed gender hierarchy. The government needed the power to restrict examinations according to sex, because, the minister explained, too many women in the higher grades would prejudice the training of the class, and that class would be off track:

> [If] five women were to be appointed out of six vacancies the result of that in existing circumstances would be that the entrants to these offices probably would not have been given proper work and not given the opportunity and training that people of this grade should be given.[16]

It was particularly important, according to the minister, that the junior administrative grades, the grades from which the majority of the heads of departments emerged, not be placed in this difficulty.[17] I believe the minister thought all women would get married and leave the civil service. Once again, women's participation in the public sphere was seen to bring chaos, to disrupt the 'normal and natural' flow of the system.

15 *DD*, 25 Nov. 1925, vol. 13, col. 867. Ireland was not alone in restricting women's positions in the civil service. In the 1919 reorganization of the British civil service, women were excluded from positions above the clerical level. Feminists protested and succeeded in 'obtaining a parliamentary resolution directing the Treasury Department to grant women equal opportunities, but while appearing to implement this new policy, Treasury officials ensured that few women were successful. The publicity devoted to the handful of females appointed helped obscure the extent to which the post-war decade brought a restoration of prewar patterns of sex segregation in employment in the civil service, and elsewhere.' Harold Smith, *British feminism in the 20th century* (Aldershot, 1990), p. 53.   16 *DD*, 25 Nov. 1925, vol. 13, col. 863. See also, *SD*, 17 Dec. 1925, vol. 6, col. 263.   17 *DD*, 25 Nov. 1925, vol. 13, col. 863.

The minister went on to explain what the re-establishment of the traditional gender hierarchy required in this particular case. It was not only a question of restricting women's access to certain areas, but men's opportunities had to be limited as well – albeit not in quite the same fashion. The minister's plan was to confine certain examinations to women and exclude men from the positions of 'short-hand typists ... and telephonists and any classes of that sort'.[18] If this order were followed, each sex would be in positions for which they were naturally suited because the minister believed that 'women were more suitable for typing work or work of that character than men'.[19]

Suitability for jobs was one issue. Similar to this was the concern that it was unseemly – out of the natural order of the gender hierarchy – to allow women to be in positions where they would 'be controlling men of mature years'.[20] Clearly, the reverse order, which placed men in positions of power and relegated women to the lowest level of employment, was one that the minister unabashedly accepted and promulgated and one that was in accordance with accepted gender hierarchy of the time.

Another question that was central to the debate was finance. If men went into what were defined as women's jobs, the government believed that the men would demand more money, as these jobs were among the lowest-paid grades.[21] The implication was that the government, because of its belief that men as breadwinners were entitled to higher rates of pay, would acquiesce in this demand and any changes would skew the existing financial arrangements.

A corollary to this view was the belief that women were only temporary employees in the civil service because, once married, they were not retained.[22] According to one Senator, this again was simply the natural order of life: 'We all know that if a woman marries she expects her husband to support her – why should she work herself?'[23] In the eyes of

---

18 *DD*, 18 Nov. 1925, vol. 13, col. 505.   19 *SD*, 17 Dec. 1925, vol. 6, cols 247–8.   20 *DD*, 25 Nov. 1925, vol. 13, col. 863.   21 *DD*, 25 Nov. 1925, vol. 13, col. 874; *SD*, 17 Dec. 1925, vol. 6, cols 247–8.   22 This seems to have been the custom and was only given the force of law later during the 1930s. During the 1925 debate, Mr Blythe simply said: '[M]arried women are not retained in the Civil Service.' *SD*, 17 Dec. 1925, vol. 6, col. 254. During the 1930s, in a general enquiry into the civil service, the minister was asked whether it was law or custom that women were not allowed to continue to work after marriage. The minister simply replied 'Yes'. Commission of Inquiry into the Civil Service, 1932–5, R.54/2, NLI.   23 *SD*, 17 Dec. 1925, vol. 6, col. 254.

the minister, marriage meant that 'there is a greater wastage amongst the women staff than amongst the men'.[24] Why should the government spend money and time in training women who would only leave after a few years and not progress through the higher levels of the civil service? The prospect of marriage was thus counterpoised to employment – regardless of the fact that there was a significant cohort of women who never married. As one Senator forthrightly expressed it:

> [T]he fact is that when one comes to the highest positions one nearly always appoints men, even though a woman might in many respects be better, and the reason is simply that the present social custom is that as soon as a woman gets married she almost invariable leaves her employment.[25]

It was, therefore, in the eyes of the government, 'in the public interest that we should discriminate between the sexes'.[26]

Feminists and their supporters unequivocally rejected both the government's assumptions and their arguments. Their campaign was spearheaded by two women's groups – the National University Women Graduates' Association and the Irish Women's Citizens and Local Government Association. These two groups argued for a meritocracy and for the idea that women as citizens should have unencumbered access to the public sphere. Their tactics were similar to those used in the jury-service campaigns of 1924. Women's groups lobbied the Dáil, wrote letters to the newspapers, publicized their discontent. In general, feminists disagreed on both legal and practical grounds, confronting government ministers with the realities of women's lives as well as their expectations for women's future role in the state.

As in the issue of jury service for women, feminists began their attack on the government's proposed legislation by questioning its constitutionality. The civil service amendment bill, they insisted, was discriminatory and hence in violation of the Free State's constitution.[27] As one opponent of the government's bill remarked: '[W]e, in the Constitution, have accepted sex equality, and this Bill is undoubtedly an attempt to make sex

---

24 *DD*, 18 Nov. 1925, vol. 13, col. 504.   25 *SD*, 17 Dec. 1925, vol. 6, col. 253.   26 *SD*, 17 Dec. 1925, vol. 6, cols 249–50. Blythe expressed this same sentiment during the debate in the Dáil and it was echoed by others in the Seanad and Dáil. See *DD*, 25 Nov. 1925, vol. 13, col. 878 and col. 873.   27 Letter to the editor, *Irish Independent*, 24 Nov. 1925.

differentiation. As we have accepted sex equality, let us stick to it and let us not try to undermine the Constitution.'[28]

Feminists, however, went beyond constitutional considerations and appealed to an argument based on merit, on ability. In this way, they were contradicting the government's assertion that there was a 'natural gender hierarchy' that should govern society. Rather, feminists were aligning themselves with a modernizing political order that sought to move beyond concepts like natural order, providential schemes and hereditary claims.

Feminists rejected these beliefs and argued that merit – in this case, the highest examination score – should be the basis on which decisions were made. They believed that examinations should be open and positions awarded to those who scored the highest, who did the best – regardless of sex. Fitness and ability should be the determining factors, not sex.[29]

This bill was, in their view, nothing more than an 'attempt to legalize the exclusion of women ... no matter how competent or suitable, on the grounds of sex alone, from the executive and administrative posts of the Civil Service'. As such, it was 'bitterly resented'.[30] It was not, as one senator pointed out, that some posts were unsuitable for women. Rather, she thought that the word that should be used was 'unwanted'.[31] Indeed, feminists believed that women were in fact doing better than men in the examinations and that was the cause of the government's concern to lock them out of the competition.[32] It was, in the words of Senator Costello, 'morally wrong and monstrously unfair'.[33]

Feminists further rejected the government's assumption that the proper functioning of the civil service made it imperative that men not be controlled by women. They contended that 'women have proved their efficiency in the civil service, and where tested have shown themselves capable of controlling mixed staffs'.[34] These examples, in their view, undermined the validity of government claims of an innate gender hierarchy.

---

28 *DD*, 18 Nov. 1925, vol. 13, col. 525. 29 *SD*, 17 Dec. 1925, vol. 6, col. 256; *DD*, 25 Nov. 1925, vol. 13, col. 869. 30 Letter to the editor, *Irish Independent*, 25 Nov. 1925. 31 *SD*, 17 Dec. 1925, vol. 6, col. 246. 32 This view that women did better than men in examinations persisted in feminist circles. Speaking in 1935, at a meeting of the NUWGA, Mrs Kettle, a well-known feminist activist, argued that 'the replacing of examination by interview in the higher grades of the Civil Service was due to the fact that the women were beating men in the examinations'. Minute book, 1935, NUWGA, NUWGA Papers, UCD Archives. 33 *SD*, 17 Dec. 1925, vol. 6, col. 245. 34 Letter to the editor, *Irish Independent*, 24 Nov. 1925.

Those who opposed the bill also objected to legislating for all women on the basis that some women married. Why, they asked, because some women married, should all women have their job prospects limited and restricted? Just as feminists objected to the idea behind the 1927 juries bill, which legislated for all women regardless of their status, so they objected to this sweeping ban. Interestingly, they did not directly challenge the belief that married women should not work outside the home. Rather, feminists fashioned their argument to deal with the large numbers of women who never married, and whose employment prospects were being restricted because numbers of other women did.

This was a particularly telling point because the Free State had a large percentage of women who remained single. As one of the leading opponents of this bill remarked in the Dáil: '[T]he assumption that the home as a career, to be a wife and mother, is open to all those young women, is not a statement of fact.'[35] The reality was that a large number of Irish women remained single. This was conveniently ignored by the government and its supporters, however. On this issue of women in the civil service, the government legislated for all women on the basis of an idealized image of women, regardless of whether they married or not, regardless of whether they had children or not, and regardless of the age of the children. It was similar to the approach they had taken on the question of jury service for women.

Feminists predicted that limiting women's employment opportunities would have dire consequences, especially for the more educated woman. As the Irish Women's Citizens and Local Government Association argued:

> On the one hand, the advantages which the Government hopes to secure by the Bill are but a slight temporary facility of administration while, on the other, the heavy price which women are called upon to pay for the temporary facility is the total loss to generations of women of careers which it has been proved they are perfectly competent to fill.[36]

Among women's groups, the fear was that women would be forced to emigrate in even higher numbers. If women – especially highly educated women – had their career prospects so severely limited that they could

---

35 *DD*, 2 Dec. 1925, vol. 13, col. 1096.   **36** Letter to the editor, *Irish Independent*, 25 Nov. 1925.

not even sit for exams which would allow them access to the higher levels of the civil service, then their only recourse was emigration. This point was stressed by societies represening women graduates. They believed this bill was 'sacrificing the interests of the women graduates of the University ... and forfeiting [their] confidence ...'[37]

Mary Hayden, one of the leading spokeswomen for women graduates, argued that the low numbers of women in the upper echelons of the civil service, the low rates of pay and now this new measure, would drive educated women out of the country. Is it any wonder, she asked, 'that the talented women, whom the Irish Free State taxpayers are training at great expense, are flying to England when this training is finished?'[38] Having provided young women with an excellent education, the Free State was denying itself the benefits of educated women's talents and abilities and allowing other countries – such as England and the United States – to reap the benefit of the Free State's restrictive policy.

Pointedly, feminists once again argued that women had earned inclusion in the public sphere, in this case access to all levels of the civil service, through their participation in the revolutionary struggle. Senator Jennie Wyse Power eloquently made this point in the Seanad:

> No men in a fight for freedom ever had such loyal co-operation from their women as the men who compose the present Executive Council. When they wanted messengers to go into dangerous places they did not call on members of their own sex. When they wanted auditors to go out when the old Local Government Board broke down it was women they sent. It was women inspectors that went round through all the Unions and did all the work for them in that terrible time when the whole British organization practically ceased to operate, and these are the people who tell us that we are physically unfit. I regret that this has come from the men who were associated in the fight with women who played their part at a time when sex and money were not considerations.[39]

When, it was asked, 'was it discovered that women were incompetent to fill the higher offices and that in the interest of the public service they

37 Annual report of Irish Association of the International Federation of University Women, 1931, Bridget Stafford Papers, P63/37, UCD Archives. 38 Letter to the editor, *Irish Independent*, 16 Dec. 1925. 39 *SD*, 17 Dec. 1925, vol. 6, cols 258–9.

should not be allowed to attempt to secure those positions?'[40] It seemed very much like betrayal of the promise of the revolutionary struggle.

As in 1924, feminists objected to the fact that the government did not feel it necessary to consult with any women's organization or with any women's representative. As Jennie Wyse Power pointed out:

> If this sex discrimination is to be made by a male Executive Council and by practically a male Dáil I think it very unjust. No consultation of any kind took place with any representative women on the subject.[41]

As in the case with jury service, the government certainly could have consulted any of the women graduates' associations, or individual senators like Jennie Wyse Power. Obviously, the government did not feel it was necessary to do so. Perhaps it did not anticipate any difficulty in passing this legislation, and therefore garnering support and placating resentment were not deemed necessary. Perhaps, as in the bills about women jurors, the government believed that it knew best what women wanted. Perhaps it was simply arrogance. Perhaps they simply did not want women.

The government clearly underestimated the response to this legislation. In the Dáil, on the second reading of the bill, the government escaped defeat by a margin of only five votes. In the Seanad, for the first time since the establishment of the Free State, a government bill was rejected. The *Irish Times* explained the government's difficulties:

> Its chief object was to empower the Civil Service Commissioners to exclude women from certain examinations. This was regarded as a restriction of women's rights. Hence the trouble.[42]

Feminists and their allies could take comfort from the fact that the government had been put on notice that women would not accept restrictions on their rights without a public debate.

Despite the government's difficulties over the civil service amendment bills, and despite feminist protests, the assault on women's right

---

40 *DD*, 18 Nov. 1925, vol. 13, col. 522.   41 *SD*, 17 Dec. 1925, vol. 6, col. 257.   42 *Irish Times*, 18 Dec. 1925. The Seanad only had the power to delay the legislation. It would become law after a delay of nine months unless the Seanad demanded a referendum under article 47 of the constitution at the expiration of the 270 days.

to employment continued. This time the focus was on married women teachers. In the early 1930s there was talk of the government introducing a marriage bar – that is, making it illegal for women to continue their employment once they were married. While this had been the custom in the civil service, it was now to be given the force of law and specifically aimed at married teachers – at least at first.[43]

The government's rationale was both ideological and practical. Practical objection to married women teachers continuing their employment centred on the fact that these women were part of two-income families, which undermined the concept of 'one man, one job' – particularly important during times of high unemployment. The belief was that allowing married women to continue to teach prevented the spread of employment.[44] According to the government:

> [T]he question of the economic effect of the continuance of women teachers on marriage is one that has to be taken into serious consideration by the Government. The fact that women teachers are allowed to continue to serve on marriage limits the opportunity of entering the teaching profession in the case of a large number of young people who have an aptitude for the work and, in consequence, tends to restrict the diffusion of employment generally.[45]

The argument was given a more sexist twist by one headmaster who straightforwardly claimed that he was in favour of the ban 'because men were finding it difficult to secure employment'.[46] In addition, two-income families were a source of complaint among some members of the local community, giving rise to 'irritation or jealousy which arises owing to the comparatively large combined incomes where the man and wife are both

---

43 Again, the Irish Free State was not alone in introducing a marriage bar. In Britain, despite the Sex Disqualification Removal Act, the marriage bar became standard practice in teaching, 'resulting in the dismissal of many married women teachers solely because of their sex'. Smith, *British feminism*, p. 53. **44** Compulsory retirement memorandum, 15 Nov. 1932, S.6231, NA. **45** Letter to the Most Revd Thomas O'Doherty, bishop of Galway, from S. O'Neill, acting for the minister for education, 24 Mar. 1932, S. 6231, NA. The government solicited the view of both Protestant and Catholic clergy in this matter. While individuals expressed their opinions, it is worth noting that the Catholic bishops as a body decided not to express an opinion to the government. Compulsory retirement memorandum, 15 Nov. 1932, S. 6231, NA. **46** *Irish Press*, 11 Jan. 1932.

teachers, or where a woman teacher is married to a substantial farmer or shop-keeper'.[47]

On ideological grounds too, the government objected to married women teachers. Married women working outside the home violated the prevailing gender ideology of domesticity. The government was concerned that married women would be unable to fulfil their domestic responsibilities, would be unable to take care of the home as well as manage a teaching career. Despite inspectors' reports, which maintained that married women teachers were as efficient as unmarried teachers, the government believed that, 'Generally speaking, it is felt that the continuance of women on marriage must mean some loss either to the school or to the home.'

There were also questions about the propriety of married women teaching in mixed schools. The issue in this instance was not, of course, that women married. Rather the concern was that they became pregnant, an obvious and noticeable demonstration of their sexuality that some at least would have preferred to have kept hidden. Moreover, those who favoured the marriage bar argued that allowing married women time off for having children disrupted the flow of the school term and might have detrimental consequences for the pupils of that teacher. The general rule was that a married woman teacher was allowed two months' maternity leave during the period of childbirth. She herself paid for a substitute teacher. The government contended that there was a dearth of qualified substitutes and that childbirth leave caused 'considerable upset to the school'.[48]

---

47 Compulsory retirement memorandum, 15 Nov. 1932, S.6231, NA. In his *History of the Irish National Teachers' Organisation* (Dublin, [1970?]), T.J. O'Connell notes that it was politics in the lowest sense of the term – the matter of vote-getting – that prompted its introduction in the first instance. 'In the latter '20s when depression and cuts were in the air, Professor O'Sullivan more than once told me of the grumbling about teachers' "double salaries", which he and other TDs frequently heard on the occasion of their visits to the rural areas. After the usual parish meetings there was the adjournment for refreshments to the local inn or in the case of ministers or other VIPs to a private residence. Not infrequently were they told that "the teacher above there with the double salary was the richest man in the parish". Mr Blythe as minister for finance thought the teachers' salaries were too high and cut them by ten per cent. He admitted and so did his successor in 1934, that he had first thought of making an extra heavy cut in the double salary, but administrative difficulties would not make this worthwhile. Both governments were equally responsible for the marriage ban and both were inspired at least partially by the same political motives.' O'Connell, *History of the Irish National Teachers' Organisation*, pp 281–2. 48 Compulsory retirement memorandum, 15 Nov. 1932, S.6231, NA.

The government's proposal met with opposition from the Irish National Teachers' Organisation (INTO). In early February of 1932, their central executive committee unanimously passed a resolution opposing the proposed ban:

> That on economical, educational and ethical grounds, the Executive object to the proposed discontinuance of women teachers on marriage, and will offer the most uncompromising opposition to the introduction of any [such] rule.[49]

INTO countered the government's arguments for the marriage bar by stressing the maturity, experience and nurturing skills that married women brought to their teaching. Indeed, the teachers' organization stressed the fact that a number of married women teachers had been recognized for the excellence of their teaching, and their outstanding abilities would be lost if the ban were implemented. INTO further contended that not only was there not a waiting list of trained teachers but rather 'there have not been sufficient candidates in this country for the positions available' and teachers had to be recruited from England and Scotland.[50]

Moreover, INTO predicted that there would be difficulty in attracting the best type of woman candidate under the new conditions and that 'women will regard the profession merely as a stepping stone to marriage, the sense of responsibility will consequently be lessened and the efficiency affected'.[51] Finally, teachers dismissed the threat to domesticity that married women teachers supposedly posed. The home, INTO claimed, 'is not seriously affected as her salary enables a married woman to employ competent help'.[52]

INTO was no more successful in deterring the government than the feminist groups who opposed the civil service amendment bill. It did, however, win a concession in that compulsory retirement would only apply to those teachers hired after October 1933, not to its present members.

The marriage ban was eventually extended to all members of the civil service as law, not custom. It had important ramifications. Basically, the state forced women to choose between personal fulfilment and economic autonomy. As the noted activist Mary Kettle remarked: '[W]omen from

---

49 *Irish Press*, 8 Feb. 1932. **50** *Irish Press*, 11 Jan. 1932. **51** Compulsory retirement memorandum, 15 Nov. 1932, S.6231, NA. **52** Ibid.

their entry until they reach the age of 45 or 50 are looked on as if they were loitering with intent to commit a felony – the felony in this case being marriage.'[53] The marriage ban increased women's dependence on men. Its effect on women's dreams and aspirations is unknowable. What we do know is that

> it made it easier to play off groups of women against each other, married against single and older against younger, since the marriage ban ensured that the majority of working women were young. As well as creating divisions between women, the marriage ban deprived the female image of the important elements of authority and maturity. It worked to the advantage of employers to have a large group in the labour force who could be expected to be docile, cheap (having in theory no dependents) and unlikely to organise because they expected not to stay at work long. The older woman at work, especially if she had a degree of authority, was the object of some hostility from both men and younger women.[54]

Thus the marriage ban worked to secure, to strengthen, the traditional gender hierarchy of a patriarchal society.

Both the Civil Service Amendment Act and the enactment of a marriage bar were aimed at white-collar middle-class positions – women in the professions. The government, however, did not discriminate in its efforts to control and limit women's employment: it also went after working-class women.

In 1932, a Fianna Fáil government under de Valera took power. The peaceful transition from Cosgrave's government to their former adversaries in the Civil War underscored the stability of the fledgling democracy of the Irish Free State. It was a significant achievement for Cumann na nGaedheal, Fianna Fáil and the Irish army. De Valera's government included an energetic and efficient minister for industry and commerce, Sean Lemass. Destined to be a future taoiseach, Lemass seemed determined to move the Free State's economy toward self-sufficiency. He also was a believer in a meritocracy – except perhaps where gender relations were concerned, as evidenced by his sponsorship of the conditions of

53 Quoted in Daly, 'Women, work and trade unionism', p. 76. **54** Eiléan Ní Chuilleanáin (ed.), *Irish women: image and achievement* (Dublin, 1985), pp 6–7.

employment bill in 1935, which attempted to extend the government's power to cover working-class women's employment.[55]

As Bew and Patterson point out, Lemass stood above all for the principle of a 'career open to the talents': rewards were to be allocated on a basis of merit rather than nepotism or other criteria.[56] But as the clauses of the conditions of employment bill reveal, Lemass was advocating for a qualified meritocracy – one that was open to men only. How this major inconsistency could be ignored by traditional historians and biographers is astounding.

Leaving aside the concept of a meritocracy, the conditions of employment bill was, in general, heralded as an attempt to improve the working conditions of Irish men and women. It mandated a forty-eight-hour work week with one week of paid holidays as well as designated holidays throughout the year. In addition, it set out a myriad of regulations designed to establish standard minimum conditions in factories and shops throughout Ireland.

In addition to these progressive aspects, however, there was also an ominous note in this legislation. The bill gave the minister the very broad power to regulate the number of women who would be allowed to work in any given industry, as well as the authority to control the particular types of work women would be allowed to perform. The latter was an attempt to extend protectionism in the belief that there were certain jobs women were not capable of doing or which would be harmful for them to undertake. As the minister explained:

> There is no doubt that there are certain classes of work on which it is undesirable that women should be employed and for which they are not suited. Certain Deputies from Limerick made representations to me only quite recently with regard to an institution in Limerick in which a woman is employed stoking a boiler. I do not think women should be employed stoking boilers, but, at the present time, there is no power anywhere to prevent women being employed on work of that kind and the purpose of this section

55 There are numerous biographies of Sean Lemass. Among them are Tom Garvin, *Judging Lemass* (Dublin, 2009), Brian Farrell, *Sean Lemass* (Dublin, 1993) and Paul Bew & Henry Patterson, *Sean Lemass and the making of modern Ireland* (Dublin,1982), as well as lengthy discussions in historical surveys. In the biographies and mainstream texts that I have surveyed, there is no mention of women and the Conditions of Employment Act. **56** Bew & Patterson, *Sean Lemass*, p. 10

of the Bill is to give the Department of Industry and Commerce power to make regulations preventing *the employment of women on any class of work on which it is undesirable that women should be engaged* [emphasis added].[57]

Protectionism was a highly contentious issue even among women's groups.[58] During the course of the debate in the Dáil, Lemass himself referred to the opposition to protectionist measures by some women's international organizations in Geneva 'on the grounds that they were designed to create positions of inequality as far as the law was concerned in respect of the sexes'.[59] It was an argument Lemass did not accept. Rather, he opted for the power to decide what work was – and was not – appropriate work for women. It was a sentiment worthy of Cumann nGaedheal and Kevin O'Higgins. Once again, the government knew what was best for women.

Protectionism was not the only problematic section of the legislation. What also concerned feminists with the conditions of employment bill was the power given to the minister to regulate the number of women involved in any given industry. The rationale behind this section was clear: it was fear that women were taking over men's jobs. When the bill was being discussed in cabinet, the minister explained the necessity for this section to his colleagues:

> [I]f employment is to be balanced in the Saorstat, certain avenues must be reserved for men. In other countries, employment is given to men in heavy industries, heavy engineering, manufacture of machinery, ... manufacture of steel, ... In the Saorstat heavy industries are not at present carried on to an appreciable extent, the Minister is convinced of the necessity for statutory prohibition, for without it, women may rapidly be recruited for most classes of industry that are likely to be developed here.[60]

57 *DD*, 17 May 1935, vol. 56, col. 1280.   58 In the United States, for example, the women's movement split over the issue of protection. The National Women's Party opposed protective legislation, seeing it as undermining women's claim for equality and their quest for an equal rights amendment, while the League of Women Voters supported protective legislation as necessary to protect women from unsafe and unhealthy working conditions.   59 *DD*, 26 June 1935, vol. 57, cols 1072–3.   60 Memorandum from the department of industry and commerce to members of the executive council, 2 Oct. 1933, S.6462A, NA.

The minister voiced the concern of some members of the government, of the legislature, as well as a significant section of the labour movement. They believed that women were replacing men in various trades and industries. In the Dáil, the minister spoke of the 'invasion of industry by women'. He went on to say:

> [T]here are industries at the present time in which men only are employed, and in respect to which, nevertheless, developments are taking place which may make it possible for women to do the work these men are now doing. If these developments occur, I think it is desirable that we should have power, when we deem it necessary to use it after consultation with the interested parties, to ensure that men will continue to be employed. We have had a case of that kind only quite recently in certain industries where the general adoption of certain machines resulted in the employment of women to do work which men had previously regarded as their own.[61]

The reason for the changeover to employing women was simple. On the whole, women workers were willing to work for less, to accept lower wages than men. The minister explained this phenomenon in terms of general gender differences:

> [W]omen as a class are prepared to work for less wages: first, because, the average woman going into industry does not consider that she is going into an occupation which is going to maintain her for the rest of her life, while a man, when he grows up and seeks industrial work, does so with the knowledge that he is going to work all his life and, consequently, is concerned to ensure that the conditions of his work and the wages he will get will be such as will enable him to live his life in full, whereas the average woman only regards the employment she gets as a means of livelihood until matrimony.[62]

The minister failed to note that many times married women did not have a choice in whether they wished to work after marriage. Often their decisions were dictated by government policy and industrial custom.

61 *DD*, 26 June 1935, vol. 57, col. 1074.   62 *SD*, 12 Dec. 1935, vol. 20, col. 1423.

Undeterred by the lack of complexity in his remarks, the minister continued his explanation:

> Secondly, and because of that, the great majority of women in industry are single, while on the other hand, the great majority of men are married, and the standard of living whereby the average single woman would be able to maintain herself would not be sufficient to enable the average male employee to maintain himself, because the male employee has got, in the average case, dependents to be supported out of his wage, and on that account the general standard of women's wages will be lower than the general standard of men's wages.[63]

Like his predecessor, the minister glossed over the important detail that in many cases, single women were supporting parents or other family members either as a sole support or as a necessary contributor to the family's survival. Not surprisingly, in the climate of the times, the suggestion that the government support equal wages for men and women was dismissed by the minister. He predicted that such an idea would lead to a lowering of men's wages and a decrease in women's employment.[64]

What emerged from this debate was that, for those who supported the bill, the right to employment was a man's right that needed to be protected from the upsurge of women workers. In the Dáil, the Labour Party supported the gender provisions of the bill. The only significant comment made by the leadership of the party was a discussion of how women had replaced men in the clothing industry.[65] Indeed, Lemass claimed that he had 'received resolutions passed by various labour organisations lately, male labour organisations, urging that this section of the Bill [restricting women's employment] should be used drastically ...'[66]

The underlying feeling and disquiet that permeated the discussion was expressed directly by one of the leaders of the main opposition party, Fine Gael. Deputy McGilligan believed the bill was a reaction against 'the modern tendency to give women equality with men'[67] and was an attempt to keep for men the privileges they had long enjoyed. He asked his colleagues to admit that what they were really saying was

63 *SD*, 12 Dec. 1935, vol. 20, col. 1423.   64 *SD*, 27 Nov. 1935, vol. 20, col. 1223.   65 *DD*, 26 June 1935, vol. 57, cols 1084–5.   66 *DD*, 26 June 1935, vol. 57, col. 1075.   67 *DD*, 26 June 1935, vol. 57, cols 1070–1.

that there are certain occupations which in our wisdom – in this House composed almost entirely of men – we will not allow women to enter into. Why not cut out all this stuff about humanitarianism, and say that, save for certain things, we will not encourage women to come into our territory: that what we have we will hold, according to the good old man in possession argument.[68]

This was, however, too blunt, too bald a statement for most members of the Dáil and Seanad. They preferred the sentimentality, the gloss the minister for industry and commerce put on the bill: 'and if it comes to a choice between men and women, I would say: "Keep the men working and allow the women the benefit of the leisure which comes from these technical improvements."'[69]

Women workers were not deceived by such sentiments and the Irish Women Workers' Union, with the support of other women's organizations in the Free State, led the battle against the conditions of employment bill. Louie Bennett, secretary of the IWWU, played a prominent role in this campaign. Indeed, the IWWU believed the bill to be of critical importance and devoted both time and resources to combating its restrictive provisions. The minutes of one of the executive committee's meetings demonstrates this concern:

> It was reported that since the last meeting of the Executive much had been done in connection with the Conditions of Employment Bill. Leaflets and posters had been widely circulated, and an advertisement inserted in the three morning papers, calling attention to the dangerous powers given to the Minister for Industry under Section 12. ... In order to make our position quite clear, a letter is to be sent to the Labour Party, setting out our reasons for objecting to Clause 12. There have been protests also from other women's societies.[70]

68 *DD*, 26 June 1935, vol. 57, cols 1081–2.   69 *DD*, 17 May 1935, vol. 56, col. 1283. The issue of man as breadwinner was discussed extensively in the context of the widows and orphans bill of 1935. See, for example, Mary E. Daly's various articles; Lindsey Earner-Byrne, 'Reinforcing the family: the roles of gender, morality and sexuality on Irish welfare policy, 1922–44', *History of the Family*, 13:4 (Jan. 2008); Caitríona Clear, *Women of the house: women's household work in Ireland, 1926–1961* (Dublin, 2000); and Lee, *Ireland*.   70 Minutes of the executive committee, IWWU, minute book 8, 13 June 1935, IWWU Archives.

The IWWU could not have been surprised by the conditions of employment bill. It had long been conscious of a growing hostility toward women in the labour force. Rumours of government action vis-à-vis working conditions and conditions for employment had been rife in Dublin since 1933. Originally, the discussion had centred on revising the existing Factories and Workshops Code and the IWWU confidently expected that the minister would seek their views and opinions. Early in 1935, the secretary of the IWWU was instructed by the executive to write to Lemass, asking the minister to receive 'a deputation to discuss his plans re Employment of Women; ... to remind him of a promise he made to consider us before embarking on new legislation which would affect women'.[71] The minister organized no such meeting. Nor did he content himself with a simple revision of the existing legislation. Instead, he introduced a much more sweeping measure, and following the precedent established by his Cumann na nGaedheal predecessors in government, he did not consult the IWWU or any other women's organizations. Indeed, paralleling O'Higgins, Lemass 'dismissed women's protests as completely unrepresentative of the vast majority of women'.[72] A deputation of the IWWU met with Lemass only after the bill was published.[73]

The IWWU objected to such high-handed treatment. Louie Bennett publicly claimed that the minister had promised to meet with representatives of the union before the circulation of a new bill regulating working conditions. The union was very surprised to find out through the newspapers that a bill containing direct reference to women had been introduced. In response, the IWWU passed a formal resolution of protest:

> Legislation which deprives one section of the community of their free rights as workers is a form of tyranny which no self-respecting citizen can tolerate, and is a step backwards to serfdom. The IWWU refuses to accept for women a position which leaves their economic position open to exploitation.[74]

In seconding the resolution, Helena Molony characterized the bill as 'a drastic attack on the rights and liberties of women'.[75] And Louie Bennett predicted that, as a result of the gendered provisions in this bill, 'women

---

71 Ibid. 72 Rosemary Cullen Owens, *Louie Bennett* (Cork, 2001), p. 87. 73 *Irish Independent*, 23 May 1935. 74 *Irish Press*, 9 May 1935. 75 Ibid.

in industry would no longer be free citizens with full control over their lives and work'.[76]

Other women's groups added their support. The Irish Matrons' Association, for example, unanimously passed a resolution which viewed

> with grave concern the growing tendency of legislation to encroach upon the liberties of citizens, women citizens in particular. Section 12 of the Conditions of Employment Bill gives to the Minister for Industry and Commerce power of such an arbitrary nature as to arouse alarm in the minds of all thoughtful citizens. This Association, therefore, urges most strongly upon the Government that Section 12 be deleted from the Bill.[77]

In the summer of 1935, the IWWU sponsored a conference attended by various women's organizations on the subject of legal and industrial discrimination. Among those groups represented were the Irish Women's Citizens Association, Women's National Health Association, Save the Children Society, Mothers' Union, and Hospital Matrons' Association, as well as the League of Nations Society and the National University Women Graduates' Association. Conference delegates drew up a memorandum on the position of women in the Free State, which was sent to the Women's Consultative Committee at Geneva and to President de Valera. The memorandum 'touched on the questions of Nationalisation, Jury Service, Criminal Law Amendment and the Conditions of Employment Bill'.[78] Delegates also requested that the president receive a deputation from the conference.[79]

The deputation duly met with the president in early September of 1935. At the meeting, the women urged the president to embrace the Montevideo Treaty, which guaranteed equal rights for men and women, at the upcoming meeting of the Assembly of the League of Nations at Geneva. While the deputation was well received and although the president 'listened attentively, he could not see that men and women could be equal. He did not seem to know much about the Employment Bill.'[80] Overall, although 'Mr de Valera promised to give his sympathetic consideration to the views expressed by the deputation',[81] he did not publicly intervene in the conditions of employment bill.

76 Ibid. 77 *Irish Independent*, 11 June 1935. 78 Ibid., 3 Sept. 1935. 79 Ibid., 4 July 1935. 80 Minutes of the executive committee, IWWU, minute book 8, 5 Sept. 1935, IWWU Archives. 81 *Irish Independent*, 3 Sept. 1935.

But women would still not be silenced. Feminists held a public meeting in November in the Mansion House. Once again, they adopted resolutions deploring the deteriorating status of women in the Free State. Louie Bennett moved a resolution that condemned 'the growing tendency in this country to evade Democratic principles and to give unrestrained power to Government Ministers'. The resolution further protested against 'any infringement of equality of rights granted under the constitution and, in particular against that section of the Conditions of Employment Bill which proposes arbitrary limitations of employment of women'.[82]

Professor Mary Hayden of the National University Women Graduates' Association moved another resolution, which decried the attempt to gain employment for men at the expense of women. In seconding this resolution, Hanna Sheehy Skeffington lashed out at the government: 'It was an immoral thing to drive young women, with dependents, out of jobs to seek an alternative. Men who displaced women under these circumstances were nothing short of blacklegs.'[83] She saw the bill as an attempt 'to displace women by adult male labour ... to set up a male dictatorship, to degrade women further in the labour market'.[84] At the meeting, feminists urged women to 'stand up to the government', arguing that 'it should never be said that they accepted serfdom without a struggle'.[85] The debate in 1935 revealed much about the political thinking of feminists in the Free State. In the memorandum prepared for the Irish Women's Organisation at the League of Nations in Geneva, the claim was certainly made for equal rights for men and women. But it went beyond this basic assertion to demanding equal opportunities for men and women 'to develop their lives and their talents'. Women, the memorandum stated,

> wish to use such freedom in the interests of the community as a whole. They desire to cooperate with men in attaining higher levels of life socially, morally, economically, and politically. They realise that such free co-operation places upon them certain responsibilities and duties as women, for which nature has specially fitted them. They accept the care of the home and family as the chief of these responsibilities but hold that under modern conditions

82 Ibid., 21 Nov. 1935.   83 Ibid.   84 Hanna Sheehy Skeffington Papers, MS 24,134, NLI.   85 *Irish Times*, 9 May 1935.

women's responsibilities towards home and family demand the use of her influence in public affairs.[86]

Thus, the memorandum did not reject the notion that women's primary role was in the domestic sphere but used this as justification for entry into the public sphere – an argument inherited from feminists in the late nineteenth century and early twentieth century, and also used by Irish feminists in the struggle over jury service. In this tradition, women's role as nurturer was used as the basis for claiming political rights. However, given that this particular memo was prepared under the auspices of the IWWU, it is telling that it did not confront the dominant belief about women's primary function in society or opt for a choice for women. Perhaps more significantly, it did not base its claim to equality on innate rights. Rather, it accepted that women's participation in the public sphere was dependent on her role as wife and mother. It thus reflected the ambiguous feelings some feminists had about women's role outside the home, be it in the factory, the civil service or the classroom.

There was, however, no ambiguity in the criticism feminists levelled at the government. They impugned the government's nationalist credentials, contrasting this attack on the rights of women to the nationalist heritage the Fianna Fáil government claimed to embrace. It was, feminists asserted, 'a strange proposal from a Government which declared adherence to the Republican programme of 1916 and to James Connolly's principles of equal rights for all'.[87] Kathleen Clarke, a noted nationalist in her own right as well as the widow of the 1916 leader Tom Clarke, pointedly asked government leaders how they could reconcile this type of legislation with the ideas of the leaders of 1916 – those whom they claimed to emulate. She herself based her objections to this legislation

on the fundamental objects laid down in the 1916 Proclamation. That proclamation gave to every citizen equal rights and equal

86 *Irish Independent*, 7 Sept. 1935.   **87** *Irish Times*, 5 May 1935. Feminists had systematically been disappointed in the Labour Party. Writing in 1927, Hanna Sheehy Skeffington said: 'I remember being sorely disappointed more than once (in the City Council and elsewhere) at the reactionary attitude of labour on feminist questions. I suppose I made the mistake of thinking in terms of James Connolly and expecting labour leaders to live up to his standards.' *Voice of Labour*, 3 Dec. 1927.

opportunities, and it seems to me that if you legislate against one section of the community, if you are going to curtail them in the way they are to earn their living, where are the equal opportunities provided for in that proclamation? I cannot see where they are.[88]

Once again, women who had been active in the revolutionary struggle felt themselves betrayed by their own government. Once again, it fell to Jennie Wyse Power to give voice to this sentiment:

> The temptation to this Government to follow the example of the last Government must be very great. They have introduced restrictions not on the Civil Service but on the unfortunate workers in industry. After the Rebellion, it fell to the lot of some of us to try to replace young girls who had lost their posts in industry. I had a good deal to do with that, and these young girls kept constantly assuring me: 'When our own men are in power, we shall have equal rights.' They believed that. It may have been due to their lack of experience, but it was part of their faith. I do not know how they feel now.[89]

These sentiments were also expressed in a letter to Hanna Sheehy Skeffington from Esther Roper, a woman activist, partner to Eva Gore-Booth, and friend of Constance Markievicz. She wrote:

> When, years before the Rising, Constance Markievicz helped her sister and myself in an election campaign fought in Manchester to

88 In her speech before the Seanad, Kathleen Clarke gave an interesting analysis of the relationship of feminism to nationalism: 'Senator Foran said my opposition was "Feminism gone mad." I should like to assure the Senator that I was never associated with the feminist movement. I was always in sympathy and, where I could do so, I helped it if it did not clash with the work in which I was always engaged – work for the freedom of my country. That work is not yet completed and I have always felt that I required all my mind, heart and energy for that work. Therefore, though sympathetic to the feminist movement, I never associated myself with it, publicly or privately, and it was unfair to claim that it was a feminist objection on my part. When, if it occurs in my lifetime, we have obtained the full freedom of our country it is quite possible I will then join the feminists, but until then I am a Nationalist first. I hope I will always be a Nationalist. I think it was unfair of him to use that expression and in using it, I believe he knew my objection because, to some persons the feminist – particularly to men – is a horror.' Senator Clarke's speech then continued with the excerpt quoted in the text. *SD*, 11 Dec. 1925, vol. 20, cols 1397–8.   **89** *SD*, 27 Dec. 1935, vol. 20, col. 1248.

keep for women their right to be employed as barmaids, she used to cheer us by saying, 'Wait till women are free in Ireland, then you will see that men workers will treat women workers as equal comrades, not as serfs.' Knowing James Connolly, I believed her. Then came the Rising in 1916 with its magnificent proclamation. 'The Rising guarantees equal rights and equal opportunities to all its citizens and declares its resolve to pursue the happiness and prosperity of the whole nation and of all its parts.' Never had there been such a firm foundation of justice and freedom guaranteed by any country to its women citizens. And now, alas, in 1935, a Republican government introduces a bill making women's right to work dependent on the autocratic decision of a Minister.

Speaking as a woman of the Irish race myself, I appeal to those who have suffered so much for freedom not to go back on the comrades who led them in 1916. Women, too, earned their freedom then. It would be to the everlasting shame of the youth of Ireland thus to betray those who, living and dying, gave their all to Ireland.[90]

The Labour Party fared no better than the government in remaining faithful to its heritage, according to feminists, and it was subject to severe criticism for its failure to live up to its stated ideals. Senator Kathleen Clarke chastised the party for accepting a bill that so clearly negated the principles of its founder, James Connolly, of equal rights and equal opportunities for all the citizens of the state.[91] Senator Jennie Wyse Power pointed out that 'in the very long debates in the other House, there was no standing shoulder to shoulder'.[92]

Nor did the trade unions stand shoulder to shoulder with their comrades in the IWWU. Helena Molony had organized a number of meetings with representatives of the Trade Union Congress and the Labour Party, 'but the latter had refused to put forward any amendment to Section 12 [*recte* 16]. Letters of protest had gone to both bodies'.[93]

The Irish Women Workers' Union and their supporters had argued to its colleagues in both the trade unions and the Labour Party that the bill represented a threat to all labouring people. They pointed out that

90 Letter to Hanna Sheehy Skeffington from Esther Roper, 19 June 1935, Hanna Sheehy Skeffington Papers, MS 24, 139, NLI; see also, Sonja Tiernan, *Eva Gore-Booth* (Manchester, 2012). 91 *SD*, 27 Nov. 1935, vol. 20, col. 1256; see also Clarke, *Revolutionary woman.* 92 *SD*, 27 Nov. 1935, vol. 20, col. 1248. 93 Minutes of the executive committee, IWWU, minute book 8, 13 June 1935, IWWU Archives.

there was a very real danger in giving the state, through the minister, the power to interfere in the employment of women, to give 'practically absolute power to any minister for industry and commerce at any time to make the employment of specified groups of women in industry illegal'.[94] Time and again the women of the IWWU pointed to the dangers of leaving such power within the grasp of any individual, to allow the state the power to interfere in the lives of its citizens to the extent that it could dictate who worked and who did not. As Louie Bennett pointed out:

> [T]he power it was proposed to confer on the Minster for Industry and Commerce was extremely dangerous to women workers. ... The point of greatest danger was the extent of the power conferred upon the Minister. The Minister might apparently control the employment of women in any and every industry – prohibit them from working in this industry, restrict their numbers in another, prohibit them from working on this or that machine, prohibit married women from working and women in industry would be no longer free citizens with full control over their lives and work.[95]

This kind of arbitrary power smacked of fascism, and feminists peppered their attacks on the government with comparisons to the regimes in Italy and Germany[96] and accused Lemass of aiming to establish fascism in Ireland.[97] Hanna Sheehy Skeffington claimed this new employment bill 'out-Hitlers Hitler'.[98]

In August of 1935 at a meeting of the Trades Union Congress (TUC), Louie Bennett moved a resolution that reaffirmed 'allegiance to the principle of equal democratic opportunities for all citizens and equal pay for equal work'.[99] She accused the government of trying to cripple the power of the trade unions and focused on the increasing power it was taking unto itself. She urged the TUC not to allow the government to assume the power over working women's lives that the conditions of employment bill outlined for them. The resolution passed.

At the IWWU annual convention in 1935, a resolution was passed, 'Women's Right to Work', which stated that

---

94 Letter to the editor from Louie Bennett, secretary, IWWU, *Irish Independent*, 12 June 1935. **95** *Irish Times*, 9 May 1935. **96** Ibid. **97** Hanna Sheehy Skeffington Papers, 24,134, NLI. **98** *Irish Press*, 14 June 1935, Hanna Sheehy Skeffington Collection, MS 24,134, NLI. **99** *Irish Independent*, 3 Aug. 1935.

> This Convention protests against the growing tendency on the part of Government and of the Trade Union Movement to restrict women's right to work, and calls upon the Government and the Trade Union conference to uphold the principle that Industry shall be staffed by those best fitted for the jobs, whether men or women, and shall provide a wage scale based on equity rather than sex.[100]

But others disagreed. One speaker said the leader of the IWWU, Miss Bennett, 'had painted a lurid picture of women being driven out of employment while the fact was that men were being driven out'.[101] Another claimed that 'they had too many women in industry and they were becoming a menace to the industrial plan'.[102] But it was the secretary of the TUC, Mr Lynch, who seemed to sum up the ambivalence that the male trade unionists and Labour Party supporters had, not only about the conditions of employment bill, but also about women's right to equal pay and, more basically, women's unqualified right to employment. Lynch said that

> the whole question of women in industry had been a difficult problem for the Executive. The Labour movement generally was committed to the principle of equal rights for the sexes. The question was whether the principle could be maintained in view of the fact that the increasing use of machinery enabled women to supplant men in industry to a far greater extent even than at present. The Executive, however, was definitely opposed to removing women as a class from industry.[103]

It was small comfort for women who sought to hold their colleagues to their alleged beliefs.

Members of the IWWU and their supporters tried to deal with the fears of their male colleagues by focusing the debate on the question of equal wages. All involved in the dispute agreed that there was no question but that women were paid significantly lower wages than men. This made women an attractive employment alternative to profit-minded employers and, as such, a threat to men's employment. The government's solution

100 Mary Jones, *These obstreperous lassies: a history of the Irish Women Workers' Union* (Dublin, 1988), p. 126. **101** *Irish Independent*, 3 Aug. 1935. **102** Ibid. **103** Ibid.

was the conditions of employment bill. An alternative solution was proposed by Louie Bennett and her supporters: equal wages. She argued that

> fundamentally the issue centres round labour costs, not sex. The evil tradition of employing women as cheap labour has persisted, and although they are more expert than men in certain industries they are selected in many other cases because they are cheaper. My organisation had long ago perceived the danger of a pool of cheap labour always available for simplified mechanical processes, and we have constantly urged the necessity to restrict the employment of juveniles and to raise the wage standard of women to a family income level. ... Instead of prohibiting women from certain forms of industry, the Minister ought to prohibit a low wage standard in such industries and leave it to the employer to employ those best fitted for the jobs men or women.[104]

Again, women argued for a real meritocracy. However, the idea of selection on the basis of merit was deemed too radical a solution because it called into question one of the basic tenets of the social order – a man's indisputable right to employment. If equal opportunity and equal pay in a meritocracy were actually enforced, it would undermine male hegemony in the workforce and in the home. As one supporter of the bill remarked, its real virtue was that 'it will permit of decent conditions of family life in this country' and 'establish in law a man's right to employment'.[105] It was a direct violation of Lemass' alleged belief in the principle of a meritocracy, which apparently applied to men only.

Feminists tried to ground the debate in reality by pointing out that while it was important to talk about men's unemployment and their need for jobs, it was also important to remember that women worked in the factories and shops because they had to, because they had to support themselves, and often others, and needed to earn a living. This bill was 'not only an attempt to take the bread out of women's mouths, but to starve those who were dependent upon them'.[106] Older women who lived on their own, wives or daughters whose pay cheques were necessary for the survival of the household, widows – all these women constituted a

104 Letter to the editor, *Irish Independent*, 12 June 1935. **105** *SD*, 12 Dec. 1935, vol. 20, cols 1419–20. **106** *Irish Independent*, 21 Nov. 1935.

segment of the working population whose livelihoods were now at risk. It was one thing to talk, as the minister did, about women enjoying their leisure. It was another to face the grim realities of working-class life.

Moreover, it was unrealistic to talk, as some proponents of the bill did, about prohibiting any woman over the age of 25 from working on the grounds that by that time she should be married and have a home. Senator Jennie Wyse Power asked a senator who held forth 'about the glories of the home and said the home was the place for women', if indeed 'he was about to set up a bureau to supply women with husbands and homes'.[107] Marriage was simply not an option available to, or chosen by, all women.

Feminists and their allies also tried to bring a note of realism into the debate over the issue of protection. Louie Bennett castigated Lemass for playing the 'outworn string of protection'. She claimed that

> so far as the Irish Free State is concerned, there is no evidence of women being engaged in unsuitable work. One woman stoking a furnace in special circumstances proves nothing. Thousands of women wash by hand sheets and blankets, scrub office floors, and carry buckets of coal and water up long flights of stairs and no one worries. Women pilot aeroplanes across the world and we have ceased to be surprised.[108]

This theme was further developed by Kathleen Clarke. Demanding to know the specific industries which Lemass believed were unsuitable for women, Senator Clarke claimed that if the minister was referring to scrubbing floors and if he would make the men do it instead, she would withdraw her opposition to the bill. Scrubbing floors is, she said, 'ugly, hard and badly paid ... and men do not want it'.[109]

By refusing to recognize the many and varied realities of women's lives, and because they could hide behind a patriarchal gender ideology that masked these realities, both the Cosgrave and the de Valera governments could introduce legislation that directly discriminated against women and shrank their opportunities for employment. It was 'to an extent, suggestive of dictatorship'.[110]

107 *SD*, 11 Dec. 1935, vol. 20, cols 1399–1400. **108** Letter to the editor, *Irish Independent*, 12 June 1935. **109** *SD*, 11 Dec. 1935, vol. 20, col. 1399. **110** Jones, *These obstreperous lassies*, p. 133.

Under cover of a gender ideology that stressed difference rather than equality, that glorified domesticity, the government could ignore the reality of patriarchy and force women to remain in low-level positions, compete with each other for low-paying jobs and deny any claim to women's right to employment. The effect of this legislation was, as one women's column pointed out, that 'despite the theoretical equality given to women in this country through the franchise, it is, in company with such countries as South Africa, Palestine, South and Central America, Lithuania and the Netherlands, on the black list as regards sex differentiation'.[111] Indeed it could be claimed that 'women's position in 1930 was worse than it had been five years before, to-day [1935] it is worse that it was in 1930'.[112] The cumulative effect of the gender legislation of the years after independence had made the Free State a pioneer in inequality – an inequality for which male politicians legislated and which male clerics would legitimate and sanction.

---

111 'Women's Column', *Irish Independent*, 15 Nov. 1935.   112 This sentiment was expressed by Mary Kettle speaking at the NUWGA annual dinner in Dec. of 1935. *Irish Independent*, 16 Dec. 1935.

4

The ecclesiastical sanctioning of domesticity

On the occasion of the Eucharistic Congress held in Dublin in 1932, the *Irish Press* described the Irish families who participated in this religious celebration in glowing, if exaggerated, terms:

> Last week showed many things – and one was the steel strength of our home life. Every happening had behind it its father, mother, child. The decorations – father on top of the ladder, mother handing him things – mainly fashioned by herself – and advising, children looking on. The welcome to the legate, children in the forefront, and sitting on the steps and railings, fathers together and mothers together. Fathers, smoking, not conversational, but mothers very chatty ... the children's Mass. The mother was behind every child ...[1]

Perhaps nothing so clearly illustrates the prescriptive ideal of family – complete with its stereotypical assumptions about gender and gender roles – than does the descriptions associated with the Eucharistic Congress. The father was clearly in charge, quiet, authoritative, exuding stability, enjoying the celebration with his family, surveying his domain from the 'top of the ladder'. The mother was his chatty helpmate – 'handing him things ... advising'. Her role had been to make the decorations and she was supporting him but clearly looking to his authority, in a subordinate position. The children were passive participants, simply gazing on. It was clear they were the woman's responsibility – behind every child, successful or otherwise, stood a determined mother.

Thus stood the family – the building block of Catholic Gaelic society. This view of the family encapsulated both Catholic teaching and Catholic aspirations. The family was the building block of the nation. Strong families meant a strong nation. Central to the 'strong family, strong nation' argument were women: women as wives; women as mothers; women as

1 'And now it's all over', *Irish Press*, 27 June 1932.

guardians of the hearth and home. This view incorporated rigid gender roles and attitudes that permeated the Free State. The church would ensure that this view predominated throughout the state.

The Eucharistic Congress, described by the historian Ronan Fanning as 'the greatest international celebration of Catholicism in the history of independent Ireland',[2] was a major event in the life of the state – perhaps with a whiff of triumphalism from a people who had historically suffered through the penal laws and the general disparagement of their faith. What it demonstrated was that Catholicism was an integral part of the twenty-six counties and its influence was a vital and significant part of the culture of the Free State. It seemed to have been a point of pride for the independent state, an affirmation of a separate identity. According to President Cosgrave's latest biographer, the Eucharistic Congress was a 'Catholic triumph'.[3] And, the highlight of the Eucharistic Congress was thought to be the 'Mass at the Phoenix Park, celebrated in front of one million people, which turned out to be the single biggest gathering in the country since Daniel O'Connell's monster meeting at Tara in 1843'.[4]

To say Catholicism was important in the life of the Free State is an understatement. The Roman Catholic church was an active and instrumental partner of both the Cosgrave and de Valera governments. As the religion of the overwhelming majority of the population of the twenty-six counties, the church's positions influenced public discourse from issues like divorce to questions of sexuality.

But it was more than that. The support of the church for the Treaty and its endorsement of the Free State was critical to the state's survival. The church's approval brought with it order, stability and legitimacy, critically important in the years after the signing of the Treaty. It is vital to remember how tenuous the Free State's political survival was in the early years. Kevin O'Higgins' phrase about the 'spectacle of a country bleeding to death, of a country steering straight for anarchy, futility and chaos' captures the air of uncertainty surrounding the very existence of the Free State.[5]

Hence the agreement of the Catholic church was crucial to the state's survival. The church halted the slide into chaos. Priests and prelates warned their followers of the dangers of the Civil War and drew many of

2 Ronan Fanning, *Independent Ireland* (Dublin, 1983), pp 129–30.   3 Michael Laffan, *Judging W.T. Cosgrave* (Dublin, 2014), p. 266.   4 Quoted in Meehan, *The Cosgrave party*, p. 168.   5 McCarthy, *Kevin O'Higgins*, p. 86.

their parishioners into becoming at least reluctant allies of the Cosgrave government. Ecclesiastical support reinforced the legitimacy of the Irish Free State and, in return, the government allowed the Catholic bishops to have a dominant role in shaping social policy, in arbitrating morality. It was a major gain for both sides. When the bishops condemned the republicans as unlawful, when they spoke of the legitimacy of the Free State government, it made a significant difference in the country. As the historian Patrick Murray points out: 'Following the approval of the Treaty by the Dáil … the new administration needed all the support it could get from the Church in the face of multiple threats to its survival.'[6] He also states that in the month following the signing of the Treaty, the provisional government looked to the church to reinforce its authority and '[i]n return the government allowed the Church to influence social policy'.[7]

Throughout the period of the Free State, the Catholic church approved the government's legislation regarding women's participation in the public sphere – be it in the civil service or in the jury box. What ecclesiastical leaders supported was the idea that women belonged exclusively in the home and that political and economic rights were in conflict with – indeed diminished – women's role in the family. Ecclesiastical discourse in the period of the 1920s and 1930s – that is, the Lenten pastorals, the popular Catholic press, more scholarly Catholic writing, the propaganda of various Catholic lay organizations – all supported, legitimized and endorsed the domestic image of women.

Within this context, there are certain themes that emerge from the ecclesiastical discourse of the 1920s and 1930s: immodest dress; modern dance, especially in dance halls; immoral literature, in particular coming from the cheap English press; the prevalence of motor cars as opportunities for sin; and women's smoking and drinking in public. Did these concerns expose the reality of Irish society? Not necessarily. If it becomes a repetitive theme, one articulated over and over again from different types of ecclesiastical sources, I would argue it would seem to represent a concern – not necessarily a reality but a cause of anxiety among Catholic clergy. The power of the Catholic church in shaping and validating patriarchal attitudes toward women would give their pronouncements an important moral charge.

6 Patrick Murray, *Oracles of God* (Dublin, 2000), p. 50.   7 Ibid., p. 60.

Both political and ecclesiastical leaders believed that the events of the Anglo-Irish War and the Civil War had allowed women to vacate their position in the home – some might even say escape from the confines of the home. Returning women to the home, these authorities declared, was essential to the stability of the family, the state, and a Catholic society. Public duties drew women away from their proper domestic sphere and gave them access to an arena in which they neither belonged nor were needed.[8]

Ecclesiastical leaders sanctioned and legitimated political restrictions against women. In advocating and supporting – indeed praising – restrictive gender legislation, Catholic religious leaders constructed a particular identity for women, a domestic identity. As the *Irish Monthly* asserted in a 1925 column, 'Notes on Christian sociology',

> Woman's primary function in society – the one for which nature has admirably suited her – is that of wife and mother. The woman's duties in this regard, especially that of bringing up the children, are of such far-reaching importance for the nation and the race, that the need of safeguarding them must outweigh every other consideration.[9]

Hence ecclesiastical leaders applauded when, throughout the 1920s and 1930s, the Free State, in effect, barred women from serving on juries, forbade them from sitting for the highest examination in the civil service, subjected them to the marriage bar and restricted them from working in certain factories.[10] Women's sphere of activity was the home, the private sphere, and it was here that they made their contributions to the state. As the 1937 constitution would so aptly state: 'In particular, the State recognizes that by her life within the home, woman gives to the State a support without which the common good cannot be achieved.'[11]

Drawing heavily from the papal encyclicals of the period – especially *Casti Connubi*, published in 1930 – and from the long tradition of the subordination of women in Catholic teachings, Catholic leaders denied women a public identity, casting them solely in terms of domesticity.

---

8 As noted, it is a truism in women's studies that, during times of revolution, women's sphere expands, and afterwards, it contracts. The Irish experience followed this example.   9 Edward Cahill, 'Notes on Christian sociology', *Irish Monthly*, Jan. 1925.   10 For a discussion of jury service, see ch. 2; for a discussion of economic restrictions, see ch. 3.   11 Article, 41.2, 1937 constitution cited in J.M. Kelly, *The Irish constitution* (Dublin, 1984).

This position was obviously important because it supported the gender legislation of the 1920s and 1930s and made the Catholic church a full partner in the legislative attempt of the government to diminish the public, political role of women and glorify and sanctify their role in the home.

The Catholic church's position on domesticity was premised on certain clearly articulated ideas. Integral to their teaching was the belief that women and men had separate roles within a divinely ordained world plan. Complementarity, not equality, was the premise of Catholic teaching.

> From the principles already laid down of the innate difference between the needs, capacities, and tendencies of man and woman, and the resulting difference of their natural functions in social life, it is clear that the socialist or radical demand for the complete 'Emancipation of the woman and her equality with man' so as to abolish all discrimination between the two, cannot be maintained.[12]

Equality was thus not a possibility.

According to the church, there were clear hierarchical divisions. Men fulfilled the demands of the public sphere; women, the domestic one: 'Outside the home and in the affairs of civil life, the functions of legislation and administration, those of justice and rule are more in accordance with the normal attributes of the man ...'[13] Women, on the other hand, found their 'natural sphere' in the home and with 'her primary social duties' being those of wife and mother.[14] It was an often-repeated theme.

Even within the home, however, women played a subordinate role and had to defer to men. Men – husbands, fathers, brothers – had the dominant and controlling authority within the home. Woman may have been described as 'queen of the home', but her authority was limited, her status circumscribed:

> [I]n domestic society, the husband is, according to the natural and Divine law, the head of the family; and the wife, who is his equal in personal dignity, and sometimes his superior in moral worth, is his subordinate, as a member of the household. The reason has been already given; the married pair form a true society; and society is impossible without a controlling and governing authority.[15]

12 Cahill, 'Notes on Christian sociology', Jan. 1925.   13 Ibid., Oct. 1924.   14 Ibid., Nov. 1924.   15 Ibid., Jan. 1925.

As the above statement makes clear, the Catholic church did not simply dismiss women as inferior to men, subordinate to patriarchal authority. Woman was man's equal in personal dignity and 'sometimes his superior in moral worth'.[16] This sense of moral worth gave women a special responsibility, a special role to play within the society. As wife and as mother, women were responsible for the morality of the home – for instilling in their children a love of God and country. 'The woman's duties in this regard, especially that of bringing up the children, are of such far-reaching importance for the nation and the race, that the need of safeguarding them must outweigh almost every other consideration.'[17]

While conferring on women a clear subordinate status, ironically, the church also laid on them onerous and important responsibilities. The family was the basic unit of society and women were responsible for family life, stability and happiness. Within the family, women would flourish, and if they fulfilled their role according to church teachings, the family would thrive. 'When there's love at home, and happiness, and comfort, and innocent pleasure, the fold who compose the family circle are only too delighted to spend their leisure hours under their own roof ... be it a mansion or the humblest room in a tenement house.'[18]

Thus, acutely aware of the dangers surrounding the Free State in terms of gender relations and the role of women – dangers that could undermine the quest for a Catholic, Gaelic state – ecclesiastical leaders argued forcefully and stridently for the return of the 'true Irish Catholic woman'. This idealized version of woman stood on a pedestal above swirling currents of change that had the potential to topple that structure and undermine the ecclesiastical vision of the new state. This demanded extra vigilance on the part of church authorities.

The use of the ideal, of placing women on a pedestal, was important because it was a mechanism for controlling women and defusing any threat the modern woman, the 'emancipated' woman, posed to the state. Putting women on a pedestal took them off the political platform. Idealizing women in the tradition of the Madonna both denied and controlled their sexuality. The ideal woman was the antithesis of the modern woman and the church reconstructed their opposition using the age-old Madonna/Eve formula, which was part of its traditional teaching. It was not new.

---

16 Ibid. **17** Ibid. **18** 'Wanted! Home makers', unsigned column in the *Irish Monthly*, Feb. 1928.

In response to the dangers of the 1920s, the Catholic church looked to the family, and in particular to mothers, to provide the basis for the new society. They believed that the character of the nation was formed within the family: 'In the Irish home, Irish history has been made. If the future is to maintain the tradition of the past, Irish home life, the very root of Irish character must be preserved ...'[19] Thus, the role of parents was critical: 'Much depends for the future of the country on the manner in which the parents fulfil their onerous responsibility in the home.'[20]

Because the home was woman's domain, mothers had important responsibilities. The church's evaluation of women's role in this respect was twofold. On the one hand, it lavished praise upon the traditional Irish mother, characterizing her as an unrecognized saint who toiled daily in selfless devotion to her family:

> Famous Churchmen have upheld Ireland's honour in the eyes of the Catholic world and won for our people the title of most faithful nation; but those eminent men drew their inspiration from the humble women who were their mothers. We never may know in this world what saints have lived in Ireland in the persons of simple countrywomen, toiling and praying through lives of secret beauty.[21]

On the other hand, it was predominately Irish mothers of old who drew praise and admiration from church leaders. Contemporary mothers, with notable exceptions like Margaret Pearse, seemed to church leaders to lack those noble and selfless virtues. These mothers were held responsible for many of the social evils that were seen to be plaguing modern Irish society.

Because of their important roles as wives and mothers, the Catholic church believed women should not be allowed to participate in the public life of the nation. Not only would it distract them from their domestic responsibilities, it very likely would bring discord into the home. This was part of the rationale the church used to justify women's exclusion from the political sphere – for their opposition to suffrage, to jury service, to a political life for women. For example, in discussing the issue of suffrage

19 'Shane Lambert' (pseud.), 'The Irish home and how to save it', *Irish Monthly*, July 1925. 20 *Cork Examiner*, 26 Feb. 1927. 21 Lambert, 'The Irish home and how to save it'.

in 1925 after women's right to vote had been enshrined in the Free State's constitution, a popular Catholic periodical claimed that it was

> inconsistent with the Christian ideal of the intimate union between husband and wife ... that they should exercise the political franchise as distinct units and be thus enabled by law even to take opposite sides on public issues. Besides, the harmony and peace of the matrimonial relations are of such importance that the Government ought to exclude, as far as possible, all causes that may disturb them. It is notorious that national and political controversies arouse very deep feelings, and frequently sever friendships; hence it would seem desirable that the State should, in the interests of domestic peace, withhold from the married pair the power to vote on these questions on opposite sides. Again, the duties of wife and mother are so exacting and absorb so much of a woman's energy during the best years of her life, that the exercise of political activities or of other professional duties would endanger their due fulfilment.[22]

The conclusion drawn from this was that a woman's 'indirect influence' on her husband and children was 'much more in harmony with her natural gifts'.[23]

With this as their premise, the church clearly did not believe that women should participate in the public sphere. During the debate over the issue of jury service in the 1920s, church leaders argued

> that married women should be called upon for the duties of jurors is manifestly inconsistent with their home duties; and that any women be eligible to act as jurors in certain types of criminal cases is contrary to the Christian ideal of female modesty. Hence it is desirable that women be exempted from that duty.[24]

According to church teachings, those who desired a public identity for women were offering nothing but false liberty, an exaggerated and distorted notion of equality of rights.[25]

Such teachings certainly made the feminist demand for full citizenship seem particularly threatening. The feminist view, said some in the

22 Cahill, 'Notes on Christian sociology', 1925.   23 Ibid.   24 Cahill, 'Social status of women', *Irish Monthly*, Jan. 1925.   25 *Cork Examiner*, 26 Jan. 1931.

Catholic church, lays 'claim to equality which is foreign to her [woman's] nature',[26] and which is based on a 'new (unChristian) conception of society'.[27] Ecclesiastical leaders saw citizenship and participation in public life as fraught with danger, not to mention a challenge to patriarchal control.

Women also had the responsibility for providing the domestic ambience that would counter the cold, calculating world of the public sphere and inject warmth, beauty and spirituality into lives of family members:

> [W]oman's gifts point to her as the manager of the household, the educator of the children, and the principal source of brightness and sympathy and love which all seek in the domestic circle. It is the woman's special function, too, to maintain a high ideal of purity and goodness among the members of the family; and to impart to the home that element of aestheticism and beauty which does so much to brighten and elevate human life.[28]

Thus the Irish Catholic woman was pure and good, with a particular appreciation for the beautiful, the pleasing. Implicit in this statement was a reiteration of the belief in woman as the angel in the house who creates a haven to which men can retreat after their sordid dealings in the world of political power and commercial dealings.

However, the times were not auspicious for translating this vision into reality. The 1920s were clearly a time of moral rebellion, of questioning the traditional gender ideology, of experimenting with new styles, new forms of amusement, new roles. The leaders of the church – from the primate of all Ireland to the local parish priest – were acutely aware of these temptations. In their view, this made it all the more critical that the Free State establish itself in a conservative, traditional mould.

Certainly, ecclesiastical leaders were aware that the First World War and the revolutionary struggle had loosened the bonds of traditional patriarchal authority. As a Lenten pastoral in 1927 stated: 'Revolution and civil war bring many evils in their train. The confusion of right and wrong, the atmosphere of bitterness breathed by the young, and license of the times, inevitably lead to widespread demoralisation, not easy to eradicate.'[29]

26 W.P. MacDonagh, 'The position of women in modern life', *Irish Monthly*, June 1939. 27 Cahill, 'Notes on Christian sociology', *Irish Monthly*, Dec. 1924. 28 Ibid., Oct. 1924. 29 *Cork Examiner*, 28 Feb. 1927.

The church was clear that 'the ideal and characteristics of the "emancipated" woman of the modern American type could not be reconciled with Christian principles'.[30] Nor could Catholicism condone the violation of gender roles that had occurred during the First World War, when women were allowed to mingle 'almost indiscriminately' with men. All of this was a dangerous 'departure from Christian precedent and tradition [which] must produce effects upon female modesty, and as a result upon the morals of the whole nation, which no possible military necessity or no supposed national good could outweigh'.[31]

It was thus important to bolster the family. Church and state believed that parents had a responsibility to inculcate into their children Christian virtues, especially those virtues necessary for the survival of the state. The *Cork Examiner* exhorted those in authority to train the young 'in the virtues of obedience, and the trait of submission to lawful authority will remain with them during their lives. On the other hand, if parental control be not exercised, the future men and women of the nation will be tarred with the spirit of rebellion and will be a danger to the Church and State.'[32]

Another issue concerning the family was whether the Catholic church was only concerned with the glorification of motherhood, with the sanctification of the cult of domesticity. It was more complicated than that, however. Throughout the 1920s, there were other clearly articulated concerns prevalent in ecclesiastical discourse that bishops and priests believed were contributing to a breakdown in Irish morality and Irish family life. Quite often, the bishops would thunder, for example, about the 'lure of exotic dances, extravagance and immodesty in dress, and the craze for hectic pleasures of every kind'[33] – all of which they believed were destroying traditional Irish Catholic life.

Women were central to this religious discourse in often contradictory ways – as symbols of the nation, as innocent victims of modern trends, and as purveyors of immorality. This level of argument was clearly anti-emancipationist, seeing in the modern girl of the 1920s and '30s the incarnation of immorality. The provocative emancipated woman was juxtaposed to the young girl who was innocent and vulnerable.

In religious teaching, women were associated with both national identity and the moral health of the nation. Ecclesiastical discourse explicitly tied together nationalism and Catholicism, arguing that a return to

---

30 Cahill, 'Notes on Christian sociology', *Irish Monthly*, Oct. 1924.   **31** Ibid.   **32** *Cork Examiner*, 26 Feb. 1927.   **33** Editorial, *Irish Catholic*, 5 Mar. 1927.

Catholic standards would bring about the return of a traditional Gaelic nation.

According to the bishops, what was at stake in this discussion was the very self-definition of the Irish people. To many in the church, one fundamental basic characteristic of Irish society, of Irish national being, was purity.[34] Purity was primarily cast as a woman's responsibility, a woman's crowning glory. Women were thus critical to Irish self-definition and any rejection of traditional standards of purity endangered Ireland's definition of self. As the 1925 statement of the Irish bishops meeting in Maynooth put it:

> There is a danger of losing the name which the chivalrous honour of Irish boys and the Christian reserve of Irish maidens has won for Ireland. If our people part with the character that gave rise to the name, we lose with it much of our national strength ... Purity is strength and purity and faith go together. Both virtues are in danger these times, but purity is more directly assailed than faith.[35]

If there were any doubt about who had to bear responsibility for this state of affairs, organizations like the Catholic Truth Society made it abundantly clear who they believed was to blame:

> The women of Ireland, heretofore, renowned for their virtue and honour, go about furnished with the paint-pot, the lip-stick, ... and many of them have acquired the habit of intemperance, perhaps one of the sequels to their lately adopted vogue of smoking. A so-called dress performance or dance today showed some of our Irish girls in such scanty drapery as could only be exceeded in the slave markets of pagan countries.[36]

Or as one bishop more moderately noted: 'They could not have a clean and noble race till woman was restored to her former dignity.'[37]

Purity was, therefore, a primary characteristic of the ideal Irish women. Purity meant sexual purity. It also meant eschewing make-up, not smoking or drinking, and modesty in dress and demeanour. Modesty

34 *Irish Monthly*, Nov. 1925.   **35** *Cork Examiner*, 30 Nov. 1925.   **36** *Irish Independent*, 13 Oct. 1926.   **37** *Irish Independent*, 28 Feb. 1927.

was an important adjunct of purity. It also was a virtue which was being threatened by revealing fashions, suggestive dances, and the like: 'The cult of sex is everywhere. Sex is blazoned on our fashion plates, palpitates in our novels, revels in our ball-rooms ...'[38]

Purity and modesty, however, were not simply about sexual behaviour. There were implications for cultural nationalism as well, especially with regard to fashion and dance. The bishops regularly exhorted mothers to dress their daughters in Irish fabrics – heavy, solid tweeds that covered rather than draped the body and in 'an Irish standard of dress instead of imitating those foreign importations which offend Christian refinement'.[39] Similarly, the bishops prodded their flocks to engage in traditional Irish dances, which were felt not to be sexually provocative and which had the added virtue that they could not be danced for long hours at a time.[40] Why, the bishops asked, 'should this ancient Catholic nation copy and ape what is worst in the foreigner?'[41]

All would be well – or at least, significantly better – if women were pure and modest, if mothers raised their children by Irish Catholic standards. The moral climate of society would be redeemed and the national culture revitalized. To women, then, fell the onerous responsibility for the moral and cultural life of the country – leaving the men free to pursue power.

Women, however, seemed to be failing in this role. What was particularly appalling to ecclesiastical leaders was that in Catholic Ireland, which they believed had a history of noble and virtuous mothers, there were now to be found mothers

> who shirked or neglected their duty to their children. ... There were mothers who preferred the fashionable and crowded thoroughfare to their own quiet home; there were mothers who preferred talking on a platform or in a council chamber to chatting with their children in the nursery ...[42]

To these mothers, the bishops said:

> Do not forget that you are Irish mothers; do not forget your glorious traditions ... Appear seldom on the promenade, and sit oftener

---

38 *Irish Monthly*, Mar. 1926.   39 *Cork Examiner*, 28 Feb. 1927.   40 Ibid., 30 Nov. 1925.   41 *Irish Independent*, 2 Dec. 1924.   42 Ibid., 25 Oct. 1924.

by the cradles; come down from the platform and attend to the cot; talk less with your gossipers, pray more with you child.[43]

Throughout the '20s, the bishops warned mothers time and time again that they were failing in their responsibilities, that they were allowing their daughters to go to dances, immodestly dressed, unchaperoned and unprotected. They were shirking their duties and imperilling the spiritual lives of their children and that of the nation.

The perception was that far from being morally pure and virtuous, the country was sliding down the road to perdition. It seemed as if the Free State was brimming with all sorts of sexual activity. Certainly, the Free State government was concerned. It pondered the truth of the popular perception of an abundance of immorality and wondered what its response should be, especially to the charges in the Carrigan Report, which alleged serious seemingly immoral sexual behaviour.

In October of 1932, a Department of Justice memorandum on the Carrigan Report concluded that there were numerous unproven allegations against the state and decided that 'even if these statements were true, there would be little point in giving them currency'.[44] This was to be the standard reply of the government on various sexual issues – like prostitution, venereal disease and the like.[45]

That was one possible response – to ignore the allegations and not give publicity to the various charges of immorality. There were other possibilities, however. The state could deny the extent of the problem – claiming that, as one senator said, the 'over-exaggerated' talk about immorality defamed the people of Ireland.[46] It could also blame the problem on 'foreign imports' – foreign newspapers (England), foreign music and dances (the US), foreign fashions (France).

All these tactics were employed but most significantly, the government blamed Irish women, whom they contended were simply not virtuous enough. The government and the church believed that Irish women,

---

43 Ibid.   44 Memorandum on the Report on the Criminal Amendment Act and the Question of Juvenile Prostitution ('Carrigan Report'), Department of Justice, 27 Oct. 1932, p. 13.   45 Diarmaid Ferriter, *Occasions of sin* (London, 2009), ch. 2 *passim*, pp 100–215.   46 *SD*, vol. 12, 11 Apr. 1929, censorship of publications bill, 1928, col. 114. For a thorough discussion of these points, see Maryann Gialanella Valiulis, 'Virtuous mothers and dutiful wives: the politics of sexuality in the Irish Free State' in *idem* (ed.), *Gender and power in Irish history* (Dublin, 2009), pp 100–14.

especially Irish mothers, were failing to observe traditional morality and exhibiting a lack of modesty, purity and deference.

The historian James Smith described the Free State's response to charges of immorality as an attempt to erect an architecture of containment, institutions in which the alleged transgressors were locked away in secret and in silence, an attempt to deny, to thwart any challenge to the national narrative of Irish women's purity, innocence, modesty and virtue.

Denial was an integral part of this church/state response. Legislation was passed – from regulating dance halls to outlawing birth control. In addition, institutions such as the Magdalene laundries or mother and baby homes were used to confine women and strip them of their sense of self-worth and classify them as sinners. Official Ireland refused to acknowledge any sexual deviation from the official narrative – sexual activity outside of marriage, infanticide or anything associated with the so-called sins of the flesh were not part of the mythology of the Free State. As Jim Smith notes, women who violated the Roman Catholic moral code, women who

> did not 'fit the model' of the Irish family cell … were excluded, silenced or punished. They did not matter, or matter enough, in a society that sought to negate and render invisible the challenges they embodied; they were sexually active when Irish women were expected to be morally pure … In a society where even the faintest whiff of scandal threatened the respectability of the normative Irish family [these institutions like the Magdalene laundries] existed as a place to contain and/or punish the threatening embodiment of instability.[47]

The growth of sexual activity seemed to some to validate the belief that the public arena wherein political and economic power resided was no place for women. Any attempt by women to leave their domestic confines

---

47 James M. Smith, *Ireland's Magdalen laundries* (Notre Dame, 2007), pp xvii–xviii. It is worth noting that the Irish taoiseach, Enda Kenny, apologized in the Dáil in 2013 for the treatment of women in the Magdalene laundries. For a first-hand discussion of the Magdalene laundries, see, for example, Steven O'Riordan & Sue Leonard, *Whispering hope* (London, 2016). This book tells the stories of Nancy Costello, Kathleen Legg, Diane Croghan, Marie Slattery and Martina Gambold.

would wreak havoc not only on the home but on the nation as well – as had become evident in the growth of immorality. As one Catholic publication noted, women have but one vocation,

> the one for which nature had admirably suited her ... that of wife and mother. The woman's duties in this regard, especially that of bringing up the children, are of such far-reaching importance for the nation and the race, that the need of safeguarding them must outweigh almost every other consideration.[48]

It was not only political duties that posed a threat to women's continued domesticity, there were economic difficulties as well. Ignoring the very important question of economic necessity, church leaders proclaimed it

> the duty of a Christian State to remedy, by prudent legislation, the abuses which have driven an excessive number of women into industrial employment outside the home. ... In a Christian State, women should be excluded even by law from occupations unbecoming or dangerous to female modesty. The employment of wives or mothers in factories or outside their own household should be strictly limited by legislation. Girls should not be employed away from their homes or in work other than domestic until they have reached a sufficiently mature age, so that they be not exposed too soon to external dangers to their modesty; and that they have sufficient time before leaving home to become acquainted with household work.[49]

A public identity that encompassed both political and economic power was thus to be left in the hands of men. It is not surprising that the bishops ignored men's responsibility for sexual activity.

It would, however, be misleading to think that the bishops were only concerned about sexual morality and Gaelic resuscitation. Much more is going on in this discussion about dress, dance, cinemas, make-up, and the like. What the prelates, the priests, the propagandists were also concerned about was the possibility for emancipation inherent in these modern amusements and the levelling effect they had on the population

48 *Irish Monthly*, Jan. 1925, pp 28–9.   **49** Edward Cahill, 'Notes on Christian sociology,' *Irish Monthly*, Jan. 1925.

in general, and women specifically. Modern dances, for example, were ones which anyone who could pay the price of admission was free to attend. Modern dress defied hierarchy and did not signify one's place in the class structure – as nineteenth-century fashion did. As one historian has noted:

> [T]he battle over fashion was also about social rank. Fashion, as Georg Simmel observed, signals the cohesiveness of those belonging to the same social circles, at the same time as it closes off these circles to those of inferior social rank.[50]

However, in the 1920s and 1930s,

> The dress styles, body movements, and beauty canons associated with them made women similar enough in outward appearance so that, as snobby mothers opined, 'you couldn't tell what sort she was until she opened her mouth.'[51]

Thus, modern dress and modern dance threatened the traditional hierarchies of gender and class of Irish society. Objections to the cinema were equally complex. Certainly, some films offended Catholic sexual morality. But ecclesiastical objection also centred on the fact that the cinema was noted throughout Europe as a very female pastime and the movie theatre as a female public space. Some argued that not only was it a female space, it was more associated with working-class women, who believed that

> In the cinema, they could take pleasure in seeing strong and beautiful women and handsome men, they could become enveloped in love stories, take pleasure in seeing women who answered back, had confidence, glamour, smoked in public and wore trousers with no mind to current predominant Irish conventions.[52]

Clearly, the women in these films were far removed from the ideal Irish woman.

---

50 Victoria de Grazia, *How fascism ruled women: Italy, 1922–1945* (Berkeley, 1992), p. 222. 51 Ibid., p. 204. 52 Quoted in Kevin Rockett, *Irish film censorship* (Dublin, 2004), p. 29.

Not only did the church object to public spaces for women, they particularly objected to those that were uncensored, unchaperoned, unprotected. Equally significant, these films vividly portrayed alluring lifestyles and, according to religious leaders, left young women 'sick with discontent at the grim contrast presented by the realities of their own drab lives'.[53] Thus young women were venturing out in a 'public space' only to be morally corrupted and culturally disaffected.

This complexity of concerns was demonstrated in the 1934 controversy surrounding the decision of the National Athletic and Cycling Association to allow women to compete in the same athletic meetings as men. This did not mean that men and women would compete in the same events. Rather it meant that at men's athletic meetings, women would have their own contests, their own events. It was a highly controversial decision. Perhaps it was even seen as a stepping stone on the road to equality.

Not surprisingly, one of the first into the dispute was Dr John Charles McQuaid, then president of Blackrock College. McQuaid sent a letter of protest to the athletic association, characterizing their decision as 'un-Catholic and un-Irish' and stating unequivocally 'that no boy from my college will take part in any athletic meeting controlled by your Organisation, at which women will compete, *no, matter what attire they may adopt* [emphasis added]'.[54] It was not, therefore, only a question of modesty in dress, but also of venturing out into public arenas that had been the traditional preserve of men. To compete in these events, therefore, would be a violation of the prescribed gender hierarchy, demonstrating quite clearly that women did not know their place.

Later that month, McQuaid again wrote to the association, explaining his position in more detail:

> It is un-Irish, for that mixed athletics is a social abuse outraging our rightful national tradition is a statement that requires not proof, but only some reflection. It is un-Catholic ... mixed athletics are a moral abuse, formally reprobated by the Sovereign Pontiff, Pius XI ...[55]

53 *Irish Monthly*, Feb. 1925. **54** Letter from Dr McQuaid to secretary of the National Athletic and Cycling Association, 6 Feb. 1934, McQuaid Papers, General Correspondence, 1933–7, Dublin Diocesan Archives. **55** Letter from Dr McQuaid to the National Athletic and Cycling Association, 23 Feb. 1934, McQuaid Papers, Dublin Diocesan Archives.

Specifically, McQuaid cites the pope's position that 'Christian modesty of girls must be, in a special way, safeguarded, for it is supremely unbecoming that they should flaunt themselves and display themselves before the eyes of all'.[56]

There is a contradiction here. At least one part of McQuaid's objection was not related to modesty – it did not matter what women wore. The pope's position, on the other hand, stresses modesty and warns against women flaunting themselves. Perhaps the common theme is about power, about keeping women in a subordinate place, in a subservient role, upholding a gender hierarchy that placed man on top. There is, however, another compelling explanation, offered by Diarmaid Ferriter. He writes that the common belief was that it was best to keep boys and girls 'apart at all times', and that this is what influenced McQuaid's reaction to mixed athletics as a 'monstrous suggestion'.[57]

McQuaid's sentiments were echoed by others in the community. The boycott gained momentum and was, within a matter of days, supported by 'nearly every Catholic college in Ireland'.[58] Some on the athletic association's board supported his objections, but for quite different reasons. For example, one member said that 'men members of the association had been disgruntled because women members who had won medals had set themselves up to be as good as the men'.[59] Under attack from McQuaid and others, the association eventually rescinded its original position and concluded that if women wanted an athletic association, they should form one themselves.

From this conflict, another dimension in the construction of Irish womanhood emerges. True Irish women are not only pure and virtuous and modest, they are also demure and deferential – not wanting to flaunt themselves, to call attention to themselves – regardless of their talents. They do not venture into the public space. They do not want to compete with men, to be on equal terms with men, but rather accept their separate and subordinate role. In essence, they know their place.

Interestingly, McQuaid offers no reference for his statement that mixed athletics is antithetical to the national tradition. He simply asserts its validity. Catholic leaders simply made the equation of Catholic and Irish and that which violated Catholic doctrine also had to be at odds

---

56 Ibid. **57** Ferriter, *Occasions of sin*, p. 173. **58** John Cooney, *John Charles McQuaid, ruler of Catholic Ireland* (Dublin, 1999), p. 81. **59** *Irish Press*, 12 Mar. 1934, McQuaid Papers, Dublin Diocesan Archives.

with the national tradition. The alliance of church and state in the Free State gave extra emphasis to the church's insistence on the subordinate status of women. Charges of being un-Irish and un-Catholic worked in harmony to keep women in their place.

Overall, the construction of the ideal Irish woman revealed much about Catholic ecclesiastical leaders in particular and Irish society in general. First, the picture that ecclesiastical discourse constructs – pure, modest, deferential, respectful of hierarchy, unassuming, content with one's station in life – represents the ideal of a pre-modern society. In societies that have modernized, the emphasis is on equality of opportunity with merit superseding birth, on a decline of deference based on hereditary status, on the creation of political consciousness, and on the growth of functional specialization. The ideal the bishops were advocating reinforced those attributes antithetical to a modern or modernizing society.

Historically, the Catholic church saw the forces of modernization as a threat to their power and influence – as evidenced in a number of papal encyclicals. The church stood for hierarchy, especially gender hierarchy. In this instance, the Irish Catholic bishops chose women as the group on which to make its stand against the forces of modernization. Because they were primarily defined in domestic, private terms, because the church believed women were more malleable – with their 'more emotional temperament and ... weaker personality', their 'natural gifts of sympathy and love', their 'keener sensitiveness', their 'special aptitude to promote the happiness of domestic life', church leaders identified women with a pre-modern way of life.

The ideal Irish woman thus represented a bulwark against modernization. As an all-male institution, the church wanted to retain its dominance and superiority. Given their views about women's inferiority and subordinate status, it is indeed ironic that the church turned to women to ward off the attack, to beat back the forces of modernization, to save what was in their view, the traditional way of life.[60]

This stance against modernization also gave added zeal to the Catholic church's anti-emancipationist position. As I have argued elsewhere, by embracing and advocating the concept of woman as citizen,

60 The Irish situation was not unique, however. Bonnie Smith, in *Ladies of the leisure class* (Princeton, 1981), makes this same point about the Catholic church and upper middle-class women in the in the second half of the nineteenth century in France.

emancipationist women aligned themselves with the forces of modernity, that is, with the ideas of a post-French Revolution modern political order which was based on a constitution, was open and democratic, espoused the idea of equality and merit, and embodied the notion of progress.[61]

This alternative vision of womanhood clearly threatened to undermine the ability of the church to use women as a barrier against modernization.

This was equally true of modern amusements and pastimes. Modern dance, the cinema, mixed athletics were associated with the emancipation of women, the desire of some women to broaden their cultural horizons, explore the physical freedom of athletics, enjoy the physicality of their bodies, break through the gender and class hierarchies that had imprisoned women for so long. These attitudes would clearly weaken women's identification with the pre-modern world.

The anti-modernization stance of the Catholic church, therefore, dictated a very narrow, very restrictive gender ideology. The dominant ecclesiastical discourse refused to countenance a more multifaceted identity for women, to acknowledge that other options existed for women outside of embodying the ideal Irish Catholic woman that the church had constructed.

But other options did exist for women. One reason, in fact, the prescriptive literature was so uncompromising was because so many women were refusing to be bound by this restrictive image. Church leaders were hostile to expanding definitions of women's role because they felt under siege, because they knew that the reality of women's experiences, of women's lives, was much more complex, much more challenging than their definition would admit.

Women's lives clearly transcended the single domestic dimension of the ideal constructed by ecclesiastical discourse. Increasing numbers were working outside the home. A significant number never married. Women continued to emigrate in increasing numbers. Women were exploring their sexuality, and were having children outside of marriage. Women were going to dances, wearing imported fashions and going to

61 Maryann Gialanella Valiulis, 'Defining their role in the new state: Irishwomen's protest against the Juries Act of 1927', *Canadian Journal of Irish Studies*, 18:1 (July 1992), pp 43–60. I am indebted to the historian Carroll Smith Rosenberg for pointing out this connection.

films – often enough for the complaint to be heard that they were never at home. Women were agitating for political rights, demanding a public identity. In essence, women were modern actors in a modernizing society. Thus, the Roman Catholic church's construction of womanhood was, on one level, a response to women's changing lifestyle – a statement of disapproval, an acknowledgment that what they defined as traditional Irish Catholic culture and traditional Irish Catholic virtues were indeed under attack.

Some of the church's pronouncements were simply ignored. The issue of birth control was one very good example of how women and men defied the church and made their own decisions about their sexuality. The Carrigan Report had stated that sexual activity and the use of contraception were widespread throughout Ireland – in rural and urban areas, in cities and villages, among the working class, middle class and upper class, among Protestants and Catholics. Moreover, it had contended that the purchasing of contraceptive devices was blatantly obvious:

> We hear evidence ... that so common in some places were such articles in use that there was no attempt to conceal the sale of them, and places were mentioned to which the supply of such articles comes regularly by post to recognized vendors. At the same time quantities of contraceptive advertisements are in circulation, and price lists are extensively distributed throughout the country by cross-Channel agencies.[62]

And yet sexuality was a key concern of the authorities.

Was ecclesiastical discourse then simply a denial of reality, a discursive attempt to create an ideal that had no bearing on reality? To dismiss it thus would be to overlook an important consequence. Ecclesiastical discourse on the ideal woman gave an important moral justification to political restrictions against women and strengthened patriarchy. For example, because women were not supposed to work outside the home, that was clearly men's right, the government need not have any qualms about restricting women's access to the highest levels of the civil service, or of giving the minister for industry and commerce the power to limit the number of women working in any given industry. Because women

---

62 Carrigan Report, Department of Justice, 27 Oct. 1932.

had no power to claim political rights and a public identity, they were effectively denied the right to serve on juries. Because bearing children was the primary and defining function of women, women were denied any access to birth-control information. Thus Irish ecclesiastical discourse about the ideal woman had very real consequences for women in the Irish Free State.

Irish ecclesiastical discourse on gender was not a unique and isolated phenomenon, but part of a general conservative movement throughout Europe. Countries in Europe were anxious about their birth rates, especially those that foresaw another world war on the horizon and were concerned about their populations being able to support substantial armies. There was also a growing uneasiness that the First World War had changed the social fabric of European society. Women had stepped in and kept societies running. Their experience and success in the public sphere made it difficult for some women to hear and accept that they belonged only in the home, that they must return to the home and participate only in the domestic sphere.

In this context, Diarmaid Ferriter has noted parallels between Ireland's experience and that of Franco's Spain. I see parallels with fascist Italy as particularly striking. This is certainly not to suggest that Ireland was fascist or to gloss over the extremely significant differences among the three countries. The point is rather that both fascist Italy and fascist Spain and the Irish Free State were all considered Catholic countries and took their gender ideology from the same source – the papacy – and hence created a socially conservative image of women. Irish conservatism, while fitting the specific needs of Ireland at the time, also emerged as part of a broader European phenomenon. It was not simply the parochial reaction of a country that turned inward after independence.[63]

In these countries, for example, women were defined primarily as mothers – in keeping with Catholic doctrine. In Italy, for example:

---

63 This impression has been primarily conveyed through the study of censorship. Noted Irish writers, disgusted by censorship and Irish conservatism, painted the picture of Irish society as inward, parochial and self-absorbed. However, once the focus is broadened, different interpretations emerge. The reconstruction of gender ideology demonstrates, as I have indicated, that Irish conservatism is part of a wider European trend. Moreover, an evaluation of the political activities of successive Free State governments reveals its desire to have Ireland play a role on an international stage – be it in the British commonwealth or the League of Nations.

[T]he way women as a group were singled out in the policies of the period depended on a vision which located them primarily in the family as mothers. ... The most concentratedly offensive initiatives were those that attempted to keep Italian women confined to a destiny of reproduction and nurturing in a family seen as the fundamental nucleus of the Nation.[64]

There are other similarities. The question of modern dress, for example, was as hotly debated in Italy as in Ireland. Involved were the same questions of modesty, of purity, and the connection with nationalism. Interwar Italy, much like interwar Ireland, was

> the natural home of papal 'crusades for purity' and of Sunday hell and brimstone sermons about slackening public morality. ... the National Committee for Cleaning Up Fashion ... led a two-year 'universal uprising' against the 'horrid vice,' the ... 'shameful wound' of indecent and scandalous dress. ... [S]everal thousand small-town girl parishioners vowed to renounce cosmetics, wear sleeves to cover their elbows, and hem their skirts no more than ten centimetres from the ankle down. ... By the late 1920s, major Italian churches has posted signs barring 'immodest dress.'[65]

Compare the Italian experience to the Irish Mary Immaculate Modest Dress and Deportment Crusade founded in 1927. The MDDC – as it was known – was aimed at 'stamping out what is mannish and immodest, and encourages girls to dress tastefully and becomingly'. Accordingly, its rules asked girls not to wear short or suggestive dresses, not to bare their arms or wear attire that was sexually provocative. In particular, girls were asked to cover their knees and their elbows, and eschew those styles cut low at the neck so as to reveal their collarbone or their back. In addition, it cautioned against wearing stockings 'in shades that suggest the nude'.[66]

The MDCC also had suggestions about deportment. It asked its members to abstain from 'Smoking, Immodest attitudes and Loud Talking or boisterous laughter in public and coarse or irreverent exclamations'.[67] It

64 Lesley Caldwell, 'Reproducers of the nation: women and the family in fascist policy' in David Forgacs (ed.), *Rethinking Italian fascism* (London, 1986), pp 110–11. 65 De Grazia, *How fascism ruled women*, pp 205–6. 66 *Mary Immaculate Training College Annual*, 1927, p. 36. 67 Ibid.

also dealt with issues that were themes in religious discourse. Specifically, it exhorted its members to avoid: 'Suggestive or immodest dances; Alcoholic drink; Improper Cinema-shows, plays etc.; Anything opposed to modesty in what relates to sea-bathing, and to show one's disapproval of the same.'[68]

A year later, in 1928, the sixty-person Crusade had become a national movement of thousands, a spiritual militia.[69] By 1929, according its own reporting, its numbers had grown to 12,000 women and girls 'preserving the beautiful ornament of modesty for which the women of our race have been ever proverbial'.[70]

Nationalist concerns also mingled with moral prohibitions in Italy as well as in Ireland. The 'horrible reptile of foreign fashion' obviously tied into nationalism. So too did the fact 'that several billion lira annually were expended on luxury imports [which] spurred campaigns to "buy Italian." Propaganda berated the upper classes for their "foreignophilia".'[71]

Similarities are apparent also on the question of athletics. Initially, the fascists had supported women's participation in athletics. However, when the emancipationist implications became apparent and when the papacy condemned it in 1928, the fascists changed their position. Mussolini even demanded that 'Italian women give up even the mildest athletic pursuits as being too virile'.[72]

Moreover, as in Ireland, ecclesiastical discourse was used as moral justification for restrictions against women. Defining women primarily as mothers and wives 'provided the justification for the introduction of severely restrictive policies for the vast masses of women'.[73] Thus, under fascism, there was an attempt to limit women's participation in the work-force. In 1927, fascist Italy cut women's salaries 50 per cent. In the 1930s, the share of women working in government offices was limited to 10 per cent, and women were limited to the lower sections of the civil service – typists, stenographers and the like[74] – the very jobs Ernest Blythe had singled out as suitable for women in the Irish civil service in 1925. The belief was that women could be limited to the lower ranks because this was not their primary vocation in life.

The ideal Irish woman then – the self-sacrificing mother whose world was bounded by the confines of her home, who was pure and modest,

---

68 Ibid. 69 Ibid., 1928, p. 13. 70 Ibid., 1929, p. 11. 71 De Grazia, *How fascism ruled women*, p. 222. 72 Bonnie Smith, *Changing lives* (Lexington, MA, 1989), p. 461. 73 Caldwell, 'Reproducers of the nation', pp 110–11. 74 Smith, *Changing lives*, p. 461.

who valued traditional culture, especially traditional dress and dance, who inculcated these virtues in her daughters and nationalist ideology in her sons, who knew and accepted her place in society – served the purpose of the ruling Irish male elite. The ideal Irish woman could also be found in cities and villages throughout Italy and Spain, and indeed, one suspects, throughout Europe – wherever Roman Catholicism reigned supreme.

Yet, in many ways, women were defying the restrictions of the Catholic church. They were exploring their sexuality, having children outside of marriage, practising birth control, having abortions and even commiting infanticide. This was not a picture that the church readily acknowledged. And for this rebellion, women were condemned.

5

Women and the issue of public identity

Throughout the late 1920s and 1930s there was a debate on what women's role in the Irish Free State should be. The question was whether women should assume a predominantly domestic identity, or a public role as well as a domestic one. It is interesting to see how the discussion evolved – even in eulogies.

Constance Markievicz died in July 1927. As noted in earlier chapters, she was a celebrated participant in the Easter Rising via her role in the Irish Citizen Army, the first woman elected to the House of Commons, the first woman minister in the Dáil, president of Cumann na mBan, member of Inghinidhe na hÉireann, co-founder of Fianna Éireann, a vital part of the labour movement, as well as an artist, philanthropist and member of the aristocracy. She was a well-known figure in Dublin political circles of the time and an important part of the circle of nationalist women.

Before her death, Constance struggled 'against that pervasive version of politics which had, time and again, failed to effect the changes she worked for'.[1] Even in death, at her funeral, politics failed her. In mid-July 1927, the Free State, reeling from the assassination of Kevin O'Higgins and fearful of possible growing lawlessness, forbade Constance a state funeral, refusing her a lying-in-state, and indeed sending armed soldiers to the cemetery to prevent her followers from shooting a volley over her grave. It is almost impossible to gauge how much sexism played a part in these decisions.

The Free State government had cause to be concerned. It was reported that when Markievicz died, her funeral was one of the biggest the city had ever seen. Included in the procession were members of the Citizen Army, Cumann na mBan, women colleagues, members of Fianna Fáil and ordinary people whose lives Constance had touched. It was an impressive gathering that was seen as a threat by a nervous government.

1 Haverty, *Constance Markievicz*, p. 227.

De Valera gave the eulogy. In it he tried to constrict and compress Markievicz's life to fit within the parameters of 'the ideal Irish woman'. He emphasized her philanthropic nature, her caring efforts and the work she did for the poor – all of which, while important, constituted only a portion of her life, of her career. They were the aspects he thought suitable for a woman. His eulogy was more a tribute to what he thought a woman should be than one which captured the complexity and militancy of Markievicz's life. He said:

> Madame Markievicz is gone from us, Madame, the friend of the toiler, the lover of the poor. Ease and station, she put aside, and took the hard way of service with the weak and the down trodden. Sacrifice, misunderstanding and scorn lay on the road she adopted, but she trod it unflinchingly. … this brilliant, fascinating, incomprehensible rebel … consumed with the fires of a burning devotion to whatever cause happened to capture her restless and enthusiastic, intellectual personality.[2]

One could be forgiven for asking where was the revolutionary member of the Citizen Army of 1916, who, with a gun in her hand and a feather in her hat, was at first sentenced to death and when that sentence was commuted, was sent to jail? Where was the militant leader of Cumann na mBan? Where was the champion of women? Where was she?

De Valera's narrow tribute drew the ire of Hanna Sheehy Skeffington. Margaret Ward recounts how she wrote 'a scorching criticism of de Valera's portrayal of Countess Markievicz as a philanthropist rather than a revolutionary'.[3]

This reproach spoke to the reluctance of the political establishment to see women as comrades, as revolutionaries, indeed, in the very way that Inghinidhe na hÉireann described them. Markievicz's independence, her revolutionary spirit, her political achievements were all seemingly ignored or dismissed. The complexity, the commitment and vibrancy of her life, the multiplicity of her activities, were all denied. Constance Markievicz was flattened out, reduced, made to conform to an imaginary, non-threatening ideal.

---

2 Lindie Naughton, *Markievicz: a most outrageous rebel* (Newbridge, Co. Kildare, 2016), p. 290.   3 Ward, *Unmanageable revolutionaries*, p. 203.

The conflict over the role of women was evident in this eulogy – for what it contained and for what it omitted. It mirrored the discord in the Free State during the 1920s and 1930s over the question of women in the public sphere. Women had played a significant part in the revolutionary struggle, but those who expected that they would continue to actively participate in the political life of the Free State were disappointed. As noted earlier, the revolutionary movement split over the Treaty and the Civil War ensued. Cumann na mBan went decidedly anti-Treaty and many of the recognizable women leaders opposed the Treaty. Some of the most passionate antagonists of the Treaty were women. This invoked a hostile reaction against women playing a future role in the public sphere.[4]

Within the Free State, where the public sphere was slowly and deliberately closing to women, the issue of women's role in society and women's relationship to the state – indeed women's citizenship – became more pressing. Would women be conceptualized as full citizens, as individuals, or only as members of the family, as mothers, as part of the cult of domesticity? Could women forge a separate public identity amid the growing demands of the domestic sphere? As noted in chapters 2 and 3, women had political and economic restrictions imposed upon them in the Free State era. Moreover, as chapter 4 explained, the Catholic church weighed in heavily against women evolving any type of public identity. Under these circumstances, could women be complete and unfettered citizens in their own right?

Perhaps. What seems obvious from the evidence is that both politicians and prelates wanted to solidify the ideology of domesticity for all women. Patriarchy would prevail. There would be no choice. Feminists, however, maintained that women were citizens as well as family members and women, like men, could have multiple identities, if they chose to do so.

A number of ideological threads can be discerned in this debate: the articulation and glorification of the ideal Irish woman; the theory of the public/private divide; and the question of equality versus difference, including the concept of complementarity and the persistence of patriarchy. Some of these ideas found their way into or were given expression in the 1937 constitution. As a whole, these were the main ways in which women were told that they did not belong in politics, did not have a place in that all-important and very powerful public sphere. Rather, political

4 See Knirck, *Women of the Dáil, passim.*

and religious elites asserted that women should remain in the private, domestic sphere. For public-sphere activities, the message was clear: no women need apply. It was a repeat of the debate on jobs.

Increasingly, women were viewed as mothers whose primary role was in the domestic sphere.[5] It was pointedly asserted that indeed it was in the home where a woman could make her greatest contribution. This issue was discussed in various popular settings: in advice columns, in debating societies and in the daily newspapers. For example, in the Solicitors' Apprentices' Debating Society, on the question of women and politics, one of its speakers roundly concluded that women had contributed nothing to politics and their biggest contribution was in the home as mothers.[6] However, in a letter to the editor in the *Irish Independent* in 1925, Mary Hayden of the Women Graduates' Association countered these assertions and made the point that it was not about what individual elected women members of the Dáil or Parliament say, 'but the influence that the millions of women electors can exercise on the candidates who seek their support at the polling booths that matters'.[7]

Questions about women in the public sphere were linked to questions of national identity – to the ways in which Irish identity was defined as different and morally superior to that of the British, and thus a justification for independence. In this view, the British were characterized as morally dubious, whereas the Irish were pure and virtuous, particularly Irish women. It was a contrast in lifestyles that reflected so much more. While it was believed that British women worked outside the home, smoked and drank in public and wore indecorous fashions, Irish women, on the other hand, were overwhelmingly Catholic and supposedly led virtuous lives. They, therefore, became the lynchpin of national identity. Discursively and theoretically, women shouldered the enormous burden of being viewed as responsible for the moral climate of the nation. What became very clear was that this was an unwelcome burden, and at least some women rebelled against its constraints.

Male politicians were undaunted in their quest for an identity that demonstrated Irish moral superiority, even if it were dependent

---

5 This was a common theme in the 1920s and 1930s. It was certainly common in Mussolini's Italy and Hitler's Germany. 6 *Irish Independent*, 17 Nov. 1925, article entitled 'Solicitors' Debating Society'. A similar article was carried in the *Irish Times*, 4 Dec. 1924 entitled 'Women in public life'. 7 Letter to the editor, *Irish Independent*, 20 Nov. 1925.

on women. They were determined to ensure that women remained in the home regardless of any dissent. If Irish women would not voluntarily conform to the very highest standards and insisted, for example, on having children outside of marriage, or even of using birth control, then they would be compelled to conform to rigorous sexual standards.

Women would be obliged to obey laws that prevented such transgressive behaviour or would be hidden away. Their sexuality would be controlled by the power of the state, their bodies coerced to fit the desired mould of national identity. To give strength to the ideal of women as paragons of virtue, Irish political leaders gave ample play to the gender ideology of domesticity, which glorified woman as mother as the ideal. It exalted women who exhibited the traits associated with motherhood as part of the construction of the ideal Irish woman.

The international context impinged on the effort to construct the ideal Irish woman. During the 1920s and 1930s the new state was defining itself and articulating its identity. In a sense, Irish political and ecclesiastical leaders were conscious that this was their 'historic moment' – a time when they could prove their worth, demonstrate their ability to govern themselves, and disprove the stereotypes and slurs that had been affixed to them during their period of colonialism.

However, as noted earlier, this was not an auspicious moment to undertake such a quest. In a Western context, the inter-war period was associated with significant social change. The 1920s, for example, were, in varying degrees throughout Western Europe and the United States, known as the age of the flapper – the emancipated woman – the age of jazz, the age of *carpe diem*. Moving women back into the home was seen as a means to thwart this new lifestyle, but it was not going to be easy.

While the external milieu in which the Irish wished to construct their independent state, to define themselves and articulate their identity, caused difficulties, there were also internal problems. The state had just come through war, revolution and a rebellion – experiences that very easily could foster an agitation against traditional morality. As Roy Foster noted in *Vivid faces*, it was a time when many middle-class children rebelled against their parents, against their rules, their decorum, their code of conduct.[8] Now the voices of conservatism wanted to pretend that this rebellion had never happened:

> In some of the confrontations one can discern the forces of Catholic piety and social conservatism asserting themselves against

the more anarchic brio of certain members of the revolutionary generation (including several women).[9]

The impudence of revolution seemed to be countermanded by the unity of prelates and politicians as they struggled to make sense of the changing times. There seemed to be clear danger signals in society. The *Irish Times*, for example, pointed out that

> Throughout the centuries, Ireland has enjoyed a high reputation for the cardinal virtues of social life. She was famous for her men's chivalry and for women's modesty. To-day every honest Irishman must admit that this reputation is in danger. ... Our first need is full recognition of the fact that today the nation's proudest and most precious heritage is slipping from its grasp.[10]

Moreover, it was not just the press who articulated this view. A government report asserted the same warning, claiming that 'the moral condition of the country has become gravely menaced by modern abuses'. Indeed, the report contended that there was a sorry state of affairs:

> that degeneration in the standard of social conduct has taken place in recent years. It is attributed primarily to the loss of parental control and responsibility during a period of general upheaval, ... The commercialized Dance Halls, Picture Houses of sorts, and the opportunities afforded by the misuse of motor cars for luring girls, are the chief causes alleged for the present looseness of morale.[11]

These same sentiments were echoed endlessly from the pulpit where priests moved from public denunciation of immorality to threats of religious sanctions if the immorality did not stop.

It appeared that the Free State was overflowing with all sorts of what was classified in the discourse of the day as 'immoral and decadent' activity. These charges went beyond a violation of religious moral teaching. They struck at the heart of Irish identity. It became a political matter. That is what made it such a potent concern.

---

8 Foster, *Vivid faces*, pp 282–3. **9** Ibid. **10** Editorial, *Irish Times*, 9 Mar. 1927, p. 6. **11** Carrigan Report.

In order not to give these sweeping statements of immorality wide spread circulation, the state decided on a strategy that was premised on secrecy and denial. As noted in chapter 4, the government blamed Irish women, whom they claimed were failing to observe traditional Irish morality. This, they said, was particularly true of Irish mothers, who were seemingly swept up in the latest fads, exhibiting a lack of modesty, purity and deference. Thus, the state decided to use its powers to legislate, to create a more moral society and, in effect, to control women's sexuality. Hence it would try to create the ideal Irish woman. There was no mention of male sexuality or male responsibility.

De Valera contributed to the effort to construct the ideal Irish woman. Indeed de Valera left us an outstanding example of this type of thinking, and expressed his endorsement of the ideology of domesticity, when in 1932, as leader of the Irish Free State and head of the new Fianna Fáil party, he delivered the eulogy on the death of Margaret Pearse – mother of William and Patrick.[12] In his eulogy, he gave voice to the dominant Irish patriarchal belief concerning the ideal Irish woman. He began by asserting:

> But for the fame of her sons the noble woman at whose grave we are gathered would, perhaps, have never been heard of outside the narrow circle of her personal friends. Her modesty would have kept her out of the public eye. Yet it was from her that ... [her sons] learnt that ardent love for Ireland and for Gaelic culture and tradition that became the passion of their lives. It was from her that they inherited the strength of soul that made them resolute and unshrinking in the career they foresaw would end in death.[13]

De Valera applauded Margaret Pearse's sacrifice of her two sons, drawing a picture of an Irish *pietà*. He claimed that 'she had once said, she knew that her boys had done right and she too had done right in giving them up for their country'.[14] According to de Valera, after the death of her sons, Margaret Pearse said her role was simply 'to hold what they upheld' – a role he claimed she filled not with bitterness or complaint but

---

12 I explore this theme in an article I wrote entitled 'Gender, power and identity in the Irish Free State', *Journal of Women's History*, 6:4 & 7:1 (Winter/Spring 1995). 13 *Irish Press*, 27 Apr. 1932. 14 Ibid.

rather with courage, charity and cheerfulness.[15] We can assume this was meant to contrast with some of the other women who seemed perhaps bitter and not content to have their family's sacrifice ignored. Mrs Pearse was the idealized Irish mother, who was satisfied being a vessel through which the dead could speak, with no agenda of her own. All of this points to a passivity, a meekness. It lacks assertiveness, independence and vitality. Certainly, it lacks the quest for a public identity. Her identity was not her own, but forged only through her role as a mother.

This particular view of motherhood was further elaborated on in an editorial in the *Irish Press* following Margaret Pearse's death. It was subtitled 'Mother of Heroes' and it stated that 'The good mother moulded the soul of her children in the historic pattern of patriotism, simplicity, humanity and simple piety.' What shone through, for these editors, was Padraic Pearse's love of his mother – 'it has been said that no race honours its mothers more than the people of Ireland'.[16]

Putting Ireland in the broader context of revolutionary states, it becomes obvious that Ireland is part of a general tradition of revolutionary activities. This depiction of Margaret Pearse placed her in the historical tradition of republican motherhood, a construct that was popularized after both the American and French revolutions. According to the precepts of republican motherhood, Margaret Pearse was, first and foremost, a devoted mother who inculcated into her sons a love of Gaelic culture and Irish freedom – a love of country so strong that suffering a martyr's death for Irish freedom, for one's country, would be a welcome sacrifice.[17] That was both her duty and her responsibility, but not necessarily a guarantee of her complete citizenship. The status of republican motherhood did not carry with it the full status of citizen in any real, public sense.

It was similar to what happened after the American Revolution: the instruction of girls was not meant to prepare them to take part in political life. Women were not citizens on a par with men in the new United States. Except in New Jersey, they could not vote or hold public office.[18] Or as the feminist theorist Carole Pateman described it, republican

---

15 Ibid. See also my discussion of this topic in my 1995 article in 'Gender, power and identity in the Irish Free State', pp 117–36. **16** Editorial, *Irish Press*, 23 Apr. 1932. **17** This view of sacrifice, of dying for one's country, was prevalent throughout Europe prior to the First World War. Pearse was simply part of this generation in his willingness to die for Ireland. **18** Marylynn Salmon, 'The limits of independence' in Nancy F. Cott (ed.), *No small courage* (Oxford, 2000).

motherhood meant that women were 'subordinate companions of citizens', not citizens themselves:

> In America, a Republican mother was excluded from citizenship, but she had a crucial political part to play in bearing and rearing sons who embodied Republican virtues. She remained an auxiliary to the Commonwealth but an auxiliary who made a fundamental political contribution.[19]

In terms of the French Revolution, 'when the rights of men and citizens were first proclaimed, women's political rights and activities were suppressed, and their place declared to be Republican mothers'.[20] It was this tradition the Irish would emulate, rendering their revolution part of a tradition of revolution, not merely a squabble to defy English rule. The Irish intent was to see 1916 as part of a larger movement. That was one reason, for example, soldiers, when fighting, had to be in uniform.

In the 1920s and 1930s, at a time when there was a debate about whether women should have a public identity, women were praised not for their contribution to the public sphere, nor for their revolutionary zeal, but rather for their domesticity, for their contribution to the home.

There were, of course, active nationalist women who refused to be banished from the public sphere. But they were the exceptions – exceptions like Jennie Wyse Power and Kathleen Clarke, for example, or Hanna Sheehy Skeffington. They were outspoken critics of the limitations of the ideal Irish woman.

Irish feminists fashioned an alternative model of womanhood. They believed that women should and could inhabit both the public and private spheres. While they did not reject domesticity, they did reject this as the exclusive identity for women. As we have seen, they protested the government's attack on women's political and economic freedom. They argued that women had something valuable to contribute to the new state, had talents and insights that would enrich the Free State.

Their view of women was a complex one, eschewing the dichotomy of women as *either* political actors *or* homemakers. Feminists saw women as individuals who could be free and unfettered citizens with rights and

---

19 Carole Pateman, 'Equality, difference, subordination: the politics of motherhood and women's citizenship' in Gisela Bock & Susan James (eds), *Beyond equality and difference* (London, 1992), pp 19–20. 20 Ibid.

responsibilities, as well as mothers and homemakers. They rejected the limitations imposed by an either/or view and astutely argued for both. In speaking on this issue in 1937, Professor Mary Hayden said quite clearly that 'women were different than men and ... women were the same as men'. They did not need to be restricted to the home, and politics would benefit from their inclusion.[21]

Feminists believed that women were equal under the law. It was a straightforward argument. The right to equality, feminists argued, was guaranteed to them under the 1922 constitution, which granted women full citizenship.[22] As equals, feminists believed that they should have both the rights and privileges of citizenship as well as the corresponding responsibilities and obligations. Like Inghinidhe na hÉireann, they spoke of woman as citizen.

Feminists of the 1920s and 1930s also added a new dimension to the equality argument by enhancing the concept of legal equality with the idea of practical or participatory equality. Irish feminists said quite bluntly that they had earned full citizenship and inclusion in the body politic on terms of equality with men by their participation in the revolutionary struggle.[23] To quote Jennie Wyse Power once again: 'No men in a fight for freedom ever had such loyal co-operation from their women as the men who compose the present Executive Council. When they wanted messengers to go into dangerous places they did not call on members of their own sex.'[24]

This argument is reminiscent of the ideas found on the pages of *Bean na hÉireann*, wherein the daughters of Éireann spoke of the common shouldering of burdens, of women as comrades. On those pages, feminists argued that their participation in the revolutionary struggle would be proof, to the very few who might need it, of women's equality. Inghinidhe na hÉireann believed in women's equality without reservation. They also thought that their male comrades shared this view. They were wrong.

Woman as citizen was the feminist view. Irish political and ecclesiastical leaders disagreed. Post 1916, they believed that Irish women needed to be returned to the home, to re-establish a traditional gender order, a

---

21 NUWGA, I/51, UCD Archives, letter to editor, *Irish Independent*, 25 Nov. 1937. 22 See ch. 1 for a discussion of the 1922 constitution. 23 Some women after the First World War made this same argument. See Grazel & Proctor, *Gender and the Great War*. 24 *SD*, 17 Dec. 1925, vol. 6, cols 258–9. See also ch. 3.

gender hierarchy that privileged men, especially married men, and saw the hearth and home as women's rightful sphere.

This patriarchal view of gender hierarchy was cloaked in the idea of complementarity. Women complemented men and thus had different attributes and skills. Equality was not mentioned. As the anthropologist Conrad M. Arensberg noted in his 1937 study of the Irish countryside, this idea of complementarity was considered 'natural', 'embedded in tradition'.[25] He further stated that: 'In this dichotomy, of course, the male sphere bears higher value.'[26]

This was the framework that influenced official thinking on the question of women's citizenship. Unsurprisingly, this gender hierarchy, this idea that what men did had a higher value, was apparent in public discussion. It certainly seemed evident in the drafting of the 1937 constitution, which sparked much resistance from women's groups.

To many, women's citizenship, their participation in the state, was directly related to their place in the home. Accordingly, as the feminist theorist Carole Pateman has argued, motherhood was the mechanism by which women were incorporated into the political order. 'Women's service and duty to the state have largely been in terms of motherhood ...'[27]

This view is borne out by the 1937 constitution which, as noted in chapter 4, forthrightly declared that 'the State recognizes that by her life within the home, woman gives to the State a support without which the common good cannot be achieved'.[28] It was in the private sphere wherein lay not only women's primary responsibility, their duty, but the place wherein they made their most significant contribution to the state.

The point was that women's citizenship, such as it was, was rooted in the family, in the home, in motherhood. Because of its relationship to marriage and motherhood, it was tied to heterosexuality and the nuclear family. Indeed this view privileged both heterosexuality and heterosexual marriage as part of the sexual contract.[29] Significantly, it was tied to women's virtue because not all motherhood was equal. Virtuous motherhood had to follow certain rules, especially those of purity and modesty – both of which were tied to Irish identity.

25 Conrad M. Arensberg, *The Irish countryman: an anthropological study* (Long Grove, IL, 1937), pp 61–3. 26 Ibid., p. 62. 27 Pateman, 'Equality, difference, subordination', p. 19. 28 Article 41.2, 1937 constitution, cited in Kelly, *The Irish constitution*. 29 For a discussion of the sexual contract see Carole Pateman, *The sexual contract* (Stanford, 1988). Diane Richardson explores the concept of sexual citizenship in 'Rethinking sexual citizenship', *Sociology*, 51:2 (2017), pp 208–24.

Women's citizenship thus tended to be situated in the family, predicated on their being wives and mothers. To an extent, women were held hostage to a domestic heteronormative ideal, which restricted their choices and their opportunities. Throughout the gender legislation of the 1920s and 1930s, culminating in the 1937 constitution, women were defined in an essentialist manner as wives and mothers, as part of a family. This set up a potential conflict between women as citizens, women as individuals, and women as members of a family and dependent on that family, a nuclear heterosexual family, for her identity and her status. This potential conflict becomes particularly evident when it is juxtaposed with the idea that the family was privileged in Irish political thought as the source of order and stability. This is stated explicitly in the '37 constitution, which vests inalienable rights in the family, and which describes the family as 'the necessary basis of social order and as indispensable to the welfare of the Nation and the State'.[30]

Order and stability were of paramount concern throughout the years of the Free State. It was not an easy time, with grumbling in the army, the Irish army mutiny of 1924, the boundary commission and the loss of the six counties, the assassination of Kevin O'Higgins, minister and public face of the Cosgrave government, and the growth of Fianna Fáil to the point of the election of de Valera as taoiseach. Despite political tensions, the church continued to focus on women: as one of the shining lights in Cumann na nGaedheal remarked: 'The Bishops here issued a pastoral recently: they are very concerned about short skirts; they don't seem nearly so concerned with perjury or murder, but there you are.'[31]

Irish women continued to be the focus of pronouncements and discussions with serious consequences. In subsequent judicial interpretations, it became clear that the concept of family as used in the constitution was one founded on marriage,[32] and from this flowed the attachment of heterosexuality. Reproductive, married motherhood was how women served the state and were incorporated into the political life of the state. Hence not just any body, any woman, could be a mother. As the feminist theorist M. Jacqui Alexander pointed out, 'not just (any) body can be a citizen anymore, for some bodies have been marked by the state as non-productive

---

30 Quoted in Michael Staines, 'The concept of "the family" under the Irish constitution', *Irish Jurist* (1976), p. 223.   31 Quoted in Reagan, *The Irish counter-revolution, 1921–1936* (London, 1999), p. 296.   32 Ibid., p. 229.

of babies and of no economic gain'.[33] Single women, for example, were clearly less valued. Lesbians – those referred to by Kevin O'Higgins as 'abnormal' during the debates on juries – were not acknowledged or seen as part of the collectivity of those pure and virtuous Irish women. It is interesting to note that among the books specifically mentioned as suitable for banning during the debates on censorship were books by Margaret Sanger and Marie Stopes about birth control, and Radclyffe Hall's classic lesbian novel, *The well of loneliness*. This is important because it is a statement of the government's fear that exposed to birth control or a serious discussion of lesbianism, Irish women might falter in their civic duty.

Virtuous motherhood existed as part of a state-sanctioned family – which was privileged and protected in the constitution. These were the women who were idealized and valued, 'virtuous mothers and dutiful wives'. These were the women who were central to the ideological justification for independence. This nineteenth-century Victorian ideal, which embodied virtue, especially purity, was the manifestation, the marker of Irish superior morality.

However, these idealized women were not the only Irish women in society. There were other Irish women who became mothers outside of marriage, who were used as a contrast to the pure and virtuous women idealized in the national mythology. As the historian Maria Luddy points out, 'the unmarried mother had become, by the foundation of the Irish Free State in 1922, a symbol of unacceptable sexual activity and a problem that had the potential to blight the reputation not only of the family but of the nation'.[34] Hence the perceived need for legislation.

In particular, the objective of this body of law – be it about birth control, juvenile prostitution or children born outside of marriage – was to ensure that women would be moral, would be virtuous, would live up to their role as symbols of purity. The unspoken yet implied belief was that, in this vital area of identity, women could not be trusted to act in what was perceived to be the best interest of the nation. Indeed it was suspected that they were failing to be the paragons of virtue they were alleged to be, and hence legal remedies were needed to ensure that they would act in a correct and virtuous manner.

33 M. Jacqui Alexander, 'Not just (any) body can be a citizen: the politics of law, sexuality and postcoloniality in Trinidad and Tobago and the Bahamas', *Feminist Review*, 48 (1994), p. 6   34 Maria Luddy, 'Foreword' in Sandra McAvoy et al. (eds), *Sexual politics in modern Ireland* (Dublin, 2015), p. xvi.

This particular need to control women's sexuality raises interesting issues, especially about the rigidity and authority of the public/private divide. Women had been repeatedly told by those in power that one of the reasons that their citizenship was limited and they could/should not participate in the public sphere was that their rightful place was in the private sphere. Certainly, the Catholic church used this as one of their oft repeated themes.

However, as was evident in the 1920s and 1930s, the barrier between the public and private was fluid and in flux. Because of this fluidity, the public was allowed to invade the private as needed. The state redefined the distinction between public and private to suit its needs. For example, there were a number of bills to control women's sexuality that became public policy. Political control of women's bodies, especially women's sexuality, was deemed necessary for the good of the state and for the preservation of patriarchy.

Throughout the 1920s and 1930s, there were numerous studies undertaken, committees formed, and legislation proposed dealing with various aspects of morality. What was obvious in these instances was that the public was invading the private. What had also become obvious is that sexual activity was widespread. Despite its prevalence, however, it did not mean that controlling sexuality, especially women's sexuality, had to be publicly discussed. The preferred method for lawmakers was to establish a committee and then try to enact their recommendations into law without much public debate. The sense was that sexuality was unseemly, embarrassing and, while it had to be regulated if the Free State were to be seen as a beacon of virtue, it did not have to be publicly discussed.

Much rested on women, on the need to control their sexuality, to place women firmly in the home. This was particularly true because women's citizenship, their place in the state, was held to be rooted in women's difference from men, in their ability to reproduce. This difference was found in their sexuality. Women were sexual beings, were 'embodied', that is, linked to nature, to reproduction, to everything the ideal (male) citizen traditionally was not. It was their bodies that embodied difference. It was their bodies that relegated them to indirect citizenship. It was their bodies that the state decided it must control.

In various debates in the 1920s and 1930s on gender legislation, moreover, the need to whitewash sexuality was made apparent in various ways. One striking example that revealed politicians' own embarrassment over the reproductive process was the bar they placed on married women teaching – a ban they justified – as noted in chapter 3 – in part because married women often became pregnant and their pregnancy would be visible as they stood in from of the classroom, obviously with child, especially in front of impressionable little boys. That a number of these married teachers who were going to be dismissed had excellent teaching records did not matter. Their obvious pregnancy made them undesirable as teachers. As did the erroneous belief that there were hordes of male teachers simply waiting to take their place.

This idea that sexuality was not a proper topic for discussion also had been made apparent in the debates surrounding the Juries Acts of 1924 and 1927.[35] As the government spokesman, Kevin O'Higgins specifically referred to the fact that often times in jury trials, evidence of sexually explicit material was presented to juries, evidence that would be inappropriate for 'ladies' to hear, much less discuss. I would argue, however, that what O'Higgins was really concerned about was men's discomfort with women's sexuality. If men viewed women's sexuality as a matter of disorder, then it had to be controlled – not discussed among mixed jurors.

Another example of the idea of male discomfort with women's sexuality was the issue of birth control. Political and ecclesiastical leaders were clearly concerned about the growing influx of imported literature on birth control coming into the country. This was deemed unacceptable. Irish male leaders believed the prevalence of birth control posed a threat to the identity of the Irish people and perhaps even to their very existence as a race. This interpretation gained currency because it was believed that the literature on birth control was being imported into the Free State by the English tabloids and by cheap English novels.

In its original intent, the censorship bill of 1926 was primarily to be about birth control, about not allowing any books, newspapers or advertisements that advocated contraception into the state. This bill was based on the report of the Committee on Evil Literature, which was clearly concerned that 'demoralizing and corrupting' literature was entering the state.[36] This served as a prelude to the censorship legislation passed under both the Cosgrave and de Valera governments.

The 1926 bill was about sexuality, but sexuality was rarely mentioned in these debates. Instead, the question of birth control was subsumed under the issue of 'race suicide'. Clearly, deputies, senators and government ministers were more comfortable talking in generalities about the possible demise of their race rather than about women's sexuality.

35 See ch. 2.   36 Report of the Committee on Evil Literature, NA, 1926, S.5381.

The year 1932 saw a change of government that put into power those who had opposed the Treaty of 1922. Although the Civil War had petered away, it still cast a very long and important shadow. For Fine Gael, the unthinkable had happened. De Valera and Fianna Fáil were now in power. From rebels to government ministers in ten years seemed like an impossible feat. The story – a very good, apocryphal story – circulated that de Valera and his party entered the Dáil with revolvers sticking out of the tops of their pockets. However, these accessories were not necessary. It was a peaceful transition of power. The military held. The Cosgrave government peacefully handed over the reins of power. Very possibly, the country breathed a sigh of relief.

Once he was in power, one of de Valera's primary aims was to erase the remaining vestiges of British colonialism. This was especially true of the clauses of the 1922 constitution that he believed the Irish delegation had signed under Lloyd George's threat of terrible and immediate war. Hence a constitutional revision, which would evolve into a new constitution, was deemed necessary.

The new constitution embodied the philosophy and beliefs of Eamon de Valera. It very clearly codified the principles of Catholicism and patriarchy. It specifically raised the question of women's relationship to the state. De Valera's view was that women should have a domestic identity only. Hence his refusal to broaden his narrow idea that motherhood was the only means by which women served the state.

In the 1937 constitution, the issue of women's rights was divided into two parts – political rights and social rights. Article 9.1.3 of the constitution stated: 'No person may be excluded from Irish nationality and citizenship by reason of the sex of such person.'[37] It very clearly acknowledged women's political rights. Thus, women seemed to be entitled to full political rights.

The articles that were concerned with social rights embodied the teachings of the Catholic church in the 1920s and 1930s. According to the historian Dermot Keogh,

> Catholic culture influenced the articles on personal rights, the family, education, private property and directive social principles. In a sense, the cluster of articles 41–45 is a petrified image of positions particular to a certain current of Irish Catholicism in 1937. A

37 Kelly, *The Irish constitution*, p. 39.

senior civil servant once heard Sean Lemass say to de Valera during the drafting 'But you can't put the papal encyclicals into the
Constitution.' However, he did do so.[38]

A biography of John Hearne – dubbed the architect of the constitution
– speaks of the 'profound underlying patriarchy' of the state that determined the character of the 1937 document.[39] And then goes on to claim
that 'The Constitution reflected the prevailing attitudes to women – attitudes shared by most men and women.'[40]

Constitutional revision was followed by the writing of a new
document. It was a long and arduous process. According to John
Hearne's biographer, the process can be broken down into four parts.
He writes:

> First, there was the removal from the Free State Constitution of
> those articles which were particularly offensive to republicans. ...
> The second stage was the establishment, in 1934, by de Valera, of
> a civil service committee to review the 1922 Constitution. The
> next stage, in 1935, was the formulation of draft heads of new fun-
> damental law. Finally, a year later, de Valera decided to draft an
> entirely new constitution and this represented the final stage in the
> progress towards Bunreacht na hÉireann.[41]

What de Valera wanted to do 'was to enact a constitution that would satisfy what he regarded as justifiable republican aspirations and thereby
secure the legitimacy of the state'.[42] As one of his biographers stated:
'De Valera knew exactly what he wanted to do with power: delete the
repugnant elements in the Treaty and loosen the British connection so as
to win the independence he had argued for since 1922.'[43] What emerged

---

38 Dermot Keogh, 'Church, state and society' in Brian Farrell (ed.), *De Valera's constitution and ours* (Dublin, 1988), p. 118.   39 Eugene Broderick, *John Hearne* (Dublin,
2017), p. 253.   40 Ibid. While I agree with this statement in theory, Broderick supplies
no evidence to support his claim. His reference to Mary Daly about present-dayism
totally ignores the group of feminist women who agitated against the constitution. A
better source, for Broderick, perhaps, would have been Caitríona Clear's essay '*Women
in de Valera's Ireland, 1932–48: a reappraisal*' in Gabriel Doherty & Dermot Keogh
(eds), *De Valera's Ireland* (Cork, 2003).   41 Broderick, *John Hearne*, p. 253. Broderick
quotes Dolores Dooley in his use of the term 'patriarchy'.   42 Ronan Fanning, *Eamon
de Valera: a will to power* (London, 2015), p. 178.   43 Ibid., p. 160.

was a constitution that established a much more independent Ireland and gave voice to his world view. He sensitively appeased religious factions so that his clause on the special position of the Catholic church was acceptable to the Vatican, on the one hand, and other religious denominations on the other.

While de Valera may have been concerned with righting the wrongs of 1922 and reasserting the Catholicism of the Irish nation, his concern with equality was less apparent and certainly less impressive. It appears that he did not anticipate the resistance that his positions on women would evoke among known politically active groups of women. It was a constitution drafted by men, for men and in the interests of men. There was no consultation with women. This fact was not lost on women. In this respect, however, de Valera was simply following the negative example of the Cosgrave government with the Juries Acts and the Civil Service Amendment Acts.

The opposition to the 1937 draft constitution on behalf of women was led by the National University Women Graduates' Association in conjunction with comparable other groups such as the Irish Women Workers' Union and the Joint Committee of Women's Societies and Social Workers. They sent memos to de Valera. They met with him. They held protest meetings. Overall, they were concerned that the political, economic and social position of women would be weakened if the phrase 'without distinction of sex' were eliminated from the various clauses. This phrase had been in the 1922 constitution. Although, as we have seen, it had not prevented the government from enacting discriminatory legislation, women deemed it an important clause that could act as a barrier to further discrimination. The question was why was even this feeble barrier missing. Was it significant? Was it an indication of legislation to come?

What the 1937 constitution brought to the fore was the equality vs difference debate. Were women equal to men or were they different from men? This question, of course, used man as the standard, which was quite typical of the period. We have seen above that women's groups refused to accept this dichotomy and asserted that women were both equal and different.

The draft constitution, however, stressed difference – especially women's ability to bear children. Given the emphasis on motherhood and the family to the exclusion of women's public role, it is no wonder that some women, and feminists in particular, protested with letters to the editors of various newspapers, protest meetings, deputations, memoranda and leaflets. This constitution seemed to be imagining woman only in the home, denying her a place in the public sphere and describing her as suffering from diminished capacity.

On the first of May 1937, the draft constitution was published in the newspapers. It was given wide publicity. It was debated in the Dáil and subsequently, on 14 June, approved by that body, 62-48. As Fianna Fáil held a majority of seats in the Dáil, this was no surprise.

In the draft constitution, women primarily objected to article 41.2.1–2, which stated that:

> In particular the State recognizes that by her life within the home, woman gives to the State a support without which the common good cannot be achieved.

> The State shall, therefore, endeavour to ensure that mothers shall not be obliged by economic necessity to engage in labour to the neglect of their duties in the home.

They also took exception to article 45.4.2:

> The State shall endeavour to ensure that inadequate strength of women and the tender age of children shall not be abused, and that women and children shall not be forced by economic necessity to enter avocations unsuited to their sex, age or strength.[44]

Some women opposed the paternalism that reeked from these articles. They wanted women to be treated as adults who were capable of making their own decisions without the interference of the state. A memorandum on the status of women written by Mary Hayden on behalf of the NUWGA to de Valera and members of the executive council, dated 23 May 1937, stated that they viewed 'with alarm the Articles in the Constitution which appear to us to menace the citizen's right to work in whatever legitimate sphere he or she may deem suitable'.[45]

Moreover, the Irish Women Workers' Union wrote to President de Valera concerning their belief that while many women would subscribe

44 Ward, *Hanna Sheehy Skeffington*, p. 325.   **45** Memorandum on the status of women, 23 May 1937, to president and members of the executive council, from NUWGA in the name of Mary T. Hayden, president, NUWGA Collection, 1/51.

to the constitution, they had real fears that it would lessen their rights. Louie Bennett, of the IWWU, wrote:

> Certain sections are dangerous, not so much for what they actually state as because of their ambiguity and the implications that may be given to them. The principle of the equality of all citizens before the law is laid down, but is then circumscribed by qualifications that are undefined and subtle, and, therefore, capable of definitions far from being in harmony with the principles of equality and liberty.[46]

This was a theme in the women's correspondence with de Valera. Aware of what was happening in Nazi Germany and fascist Italy, they wanted a clear and firm annunciation of the principle of equality. They wrote: 'And, in a period of Fascist ideology such as the world is now experiencing, normal workers cannot fail to look with suspicion upon so vague a phrase (differences of capacity) in so vital a document as this proposed Constitution.'[47] In a memo dated 23 May 1937, to de Valera and the members of the executive council, Professor Mary Hayden, president of the NUWGA, wrote: 'We regret to find clauses in the Constitution which might be a directive to future Governments to pass legislation worsening the economic and social status of women.'[48]

The conditions of employment bill passed by the de Valera government, as discussed in chapter 3, was a vivid example of the state interfering in women's employment. There was the fear that this bill set precedent, and that these articles in the constitution gave the state the right to interfere in the life of the family, especially in the area of employment. The IWWU argued that women should have 'the right to choose for herself ... the avocation she will follow'.[49] Moreover, as a letter from the executive council of the Joint Committee of Women's Societies and Social Workers pointed out there was a very real fear – one which was stated in 'propaganda here, and in other countries', that 'men shall have priority of claim to women, not on grounds of superior qualifications,

---

46 Letter to de Valera from IWWU, May 1937, NUWGA Collection, 1/51. 47 Ibid. 48 Memorandum on the status of women, 23 May 1937, to president and members of the executive council from NUWGA in the name of Mary T. Hayden, president, NUWGA Collection, 1/51. 49 Letter to de Valera from IWWU, May 1937, NUWGA Collection, 1/51.

but on grounds of sex'. This they thought 'unjust' and reaffirmed their belief in equality of opportunity and equal pay for equal work.[50]

In addition, women strongly objected to the now infamous article 41.2, which stated that it was through her work in the home that woman contributed to the state. It was through her role in the family that woman achieved her potential – not in the public sphere, not in the professions, not on the floor of the Dáil and the Seanad. The family was seen as a source of order and stability in society and was therefore described 'as a moral institution possessing inalienable ... rights'.[51]

Article 41.2.1 made the point that the home was the centre of woman's world, the institution in which she made her biggest contribution. This article states quite clearly that 'the State recognizes that by her life within the home, woman gives to the State a support without which the common good cannot be achieved'. Women's groups objected to this phraseology and suggested that that the phrase might be broadened to include other work that women did, not just having babies. They suggested that this article be amended to read: 'the State recognizes that by her work *for* the home ... [emphasis added]'.

This, they believed,

> would give recognition to the value of the work done by women in public life in the interests of the home and the family, and thereby include the large class of women who have not the mother's specialized duties within the home, but who have the specialized knowledge necessary for legislation affecting home or family. Moreover, the part played by women for the common good outside the home, in education, in social service, in culture, in workshops and on the farm, has now become indispensable to a civilized State. It is surely, therefore, invidious to introduce into the Constitution a clause which makes it appear that only the women within the home can contribute to the common good.[52]

Once again, women who opposed the constitution were saying quite clearly that women did have a right to a public identity which was

50 Letter to de Valera from the Joint Committee of Women's Societies, 24 May 1937, reprinted in Angela Bourke et al. (ed.), *Field Day anthology of Irish writing*, v, pp 165–6.   **51** The articles on the family were destined to be article 41.1 and article 41.2 in the actual 1937 constitution.   **52** Letter to de Valera from IWWU, May 1937, NUWGA Collection, 1/51.

important and valuable. They wanted it recognized that women had many identities through which they contributed to the state.

Women's groups applied considerable pressure on de Valera to make some changes to the constitution. De Valera heeded some of the protests of the women, especially the IWWU, by removing the offensive phrase 'inadequate strength' and also agreed to re-insert the clause 'without distinction of sex' in article 16 so that it read: 'Every citizen without distinction of sex ...'[53]

However, de Valera refused to budge on what would be article 41.2.1 in the actual constitution. It seemed that he was insisting that in his Ireland, women belonged in the home. Hanna Sheehy Skeffington challenged de Valera on his stance as only someone of her standing could do:

> There is no woman in Mr de Valera's Cabinet and but two in his Party. No woman appears to have been consulted by him. He and his Party are up against the entire body of organised women. ... Never before have women been so united as now when they are faced with Fascist proposals. ...
>
> De Valera is thoroughly angry and full of declarations that his words do not mean what they seem. He says he only means to honour mothers in the home and that there is now no need to emphasize equality as we have it!
>
> Mr de Valera shows a mawkish distrust of women which has always coloured his outlook; his was the only command in Easter Week where the help of women ... was refused.[54]

Sheehy Skeffington was entirely correct in her assessment that the constitution had no input from women during its drafting. John Hearne's biographer makes this very point. He writes:

> Women had no involvement in the planning, shaping and drafting of the Constitution. The central figures in the process were de Valera and Hearne. The cabinet which considered the preliminary draft on 10 March 1937 was made up entirely of men.[55]

53 Bunreacht na hÉireann, article 16, p. 42. **54** Quoted in Ward, *Hanna Sheehy Skeffington*, p. 326 from a piece Hanna wrote for *Prison Bars*. **55** Broderick, *John Hearne*, p. 252.

Sheehy Skeffington referred to a delicate area when she brought up 1916. According to the sociologist Finola Kennedy, de Valera was sensitive to the events of 1916 and considered it the reason why there was consternation among women about the issue of women being restricted to the home. Speaking in the Dáil, de Valera said:

> That [1916] may be the beginning of all my trouble. I am not saying for a moment that they may not fight as well as men. That was not the question I said I had to decide, but I said I did not want them.[56]

Was women's opposition to the '37 constitution really rooted in de Valera's behaviour in 1916? Women did not have to look to 1916 to oppose the '37 constitution. There was more than enough within the document itself to concern them. The constitution drew heavily on Irish male Catholic doctrine, which urged women to stay in the home in a heterosexual nuclear family, reproducing for the good of the nation. Thus, in essence, the constitution recognized only one model for women – a model that ignored women's different life experiences, that indeed ignored the fact that women were not a homogenous group.

As women continued to protest, a mass meeting was held in the Mansion House on 20 June 1937 under the auspices of the National University Women Graduates' Association. The purpose of the meeting was to discuss the perils the new constitution held for women and to urge them to vote against it – regardless of their party preference. Under the headline of 'Women of all Parties Unite in Challenge to the New Constitution', the *Irish Independent* left this description of the women who attended:

> It was wonderful. They kept coming in droves, old women, middle-aged women, young women, working women, professional women, girls from the Sweep and from the Civil Service, girls out of shops and offices, girls who looked like film stars and girls in tweed sports coats and without hats. They filled every seat in the Round Room, they thronged the balconies, they sat on the step of the stage. The attendants kept bringing more and more chairs to seat them, and some had to stand all the time.[57]

56 Finola Kennedy, *Cottage to crèche: family change in Ireland* (Dublin, 2001), p. 84.
57 *Irish Independent*, 25 June 1937, p. 7.

Although such an outpouring of women did not necessarily herald success, de Valera and his allies were clearly concerned. De Valera's newspaper, the *Irish Press*, cast aspersions on the women who organized the meeting – women they mocked as 'learned ladies'. Such Fianna Fáil stalwarts as Sean T. O'Kelly and Sean MacEntee roundly disparaged the meeting. Through an emergency committee statement of the NUWGA, the organizers stated that 'the sneer, the epithet of "learned ladies" is unfortunate, in view of the fact that the majority of them are graduates of the University of which President de Valera is Chancellor'.[58]

In order to appeal to the widest audience possible, de Valera had insisted that the constitution was not a party document. However, when faced with opposition, his trusted lieutenants played the nationalist card. They, for example, berated women who participated in the Mansion House meeting as lacking in nationalist credentials.

It was a ridiculous charge. The women were outraged. They proclaimed that such charges demonstrated a 'strange ignorance' of recent Irish history. They asked a pointed question: if the constitution was not a party document, why was their opposition labelled 'Anti-Government Party tactics'?[59]

The organizers listed off the names of members like Hanna Sheehy Skeffington who, among other nationalist women, had attended the meeting. Moreover, for those who were not paying attention, they reminded their critics that letters of support were read to the meeting from Senator Kathleen Clarke and Mrs Kate O'Callaghan – both of whom had impeccable nationalist credentials. In her letter, Kathleen Clarke wrote:

> I am sorry not to be able to attend the meeting as I would like to help in the protest against the attempt to take from women the equal rights and opportunities accorded to us in the 1916 Proclamation. I shall be with you, though, in spirit, applauding your efforts.
>
> The rights accorded to us in that Proclamation were the result of considered opinion ... They were not intended as a mere gesture to be set aside when or if success crowned their fight for freedom.

She was also worried about the ambiguity of language in the constitution. She said the language in the Proclamation was

58 Statement of Graduates' Emergency Committee Meeting, NUWGA Collection, 1/51. 59 Ibid.

simple, unequivocal and can be interpreted only one way, whereas the language in the proposed Constitution may be interpreted in more ways than one. Therefore, I think it is up to every Irishwoman to see that no man or group of men robs us of the status enshrined in the Proclamation.[60]

Kate O'Callaghan, in her own letter to the meeting, also compared the new constitution unfavourably with the Proclamation. Concerning the articles regarding women, she wrote: 'These Articles I regard as a betrayal of the 1916 promise of "equal rights and equal opportunities guaranteed to all citizens." They are a grave danger to the future position of women ...'[61]

In their response to Fianna Fáil's slurs, the women pointed out that the constitution, as it stood, enshrined discrimination on the grounds of sex. The NUWGA challenged those who wrote the constitution 'to show that Article 40 does not open the door to sex and class legislation, that 41 does not threaten state interference with women in their home and that 45 does not still discriminate on the grounds of sex'.[62]

Certainly, de Valera received much criticism – internationally and locally – over the clauses relating to women in the constitution. Some women's groups like the Six Point Group,[63] which had worked with de Valera in Geneva, wrote to him in June of 1937 to inform him of their 'sense of dismay' at the clauses of the constitution relating to women. They asserted that these clauses were based on a 'fascist and slave conception of women'. They further asserted that 'Ireland's fight for freedom would not have been so successful if Irish women had obeyed these clauses.' Then in a very telling phrase they said, 'You who have fought all your life for the freedom of your country can surely not wish to deprive Irish women of the freedom for which they also have fought.'[64] Moreover, even staunch allies like Dorothy Macardle expressed her unease with the constitution. In a letter to de Valera, she wrote: 'As the Constitution stands, I do not see how anyone holding advanced views on the right of women can support it, and that is the tragic dilemma for those who have been loyal and ardent workers in the national cause.'[65]

---

60 'Leaves from a Woman's Diary', *Irish Independent*, 25 June 1937, p. 7.   61 Ibid., 27 June 1937, p. 7.   62 Women's Rights Meeting, Graduates Emergency Committee Meeting, NUWGA Collection, 1/51.   63 The Six Point Group was an English group of feminists who were committed to equality with whom de Valera had worked in Geneva.   64 Letter reproduced in Diarmaid Ferriter, *Judging Dev* (Dublin, 2007), p. 247.   65 Letter reproduced in Ferriter, *Judging Dev*, pp 248–9.

De Valera did not have a strong reply to his women critics. In the Dáil, defending his position, he said:

> Let us consider this whole question of women's rights. I seem to have got a bad reputation. I do not deserve it. I myself was not conscious at any time of having deserved all those terrible things that I am told I am where women's rights are concerned. So far as I know, … there is nothing in this Constitution which in any way detracts from the rights which women have possessed here.[66]

This statement demonstrates de Valera's lack of understanding of the basic elements of equality that women were demanding. For him, self-government was what was important, 'a social programme would have to wait until after the achievement of indpendence'.[67]

The constitution was submitted to a plebiscite on 1 July 1937. The idea of a plebiscite was important to de Valera because he wanted it to be clear that the Irish people had voted for the constitution and it had not been imposed upon them.[68] It was approved by 685,000 votes to 527,000 votes, thus ending the Irish Free State.

De Valera might have carried the country with him, but he had alienated many of the women who still believed in the Proclamation of 1916, with its magnificent inclusivity of citizenship and its demand for full rights and responsibilities for all. Indeed, Hanna Sheehy Skeffington asked why the Proclamation was being scrapped for a fascist model.[69] There was no answer. The spirit of Patrick Pearse was not to be found in Bunreacht na hÉireann.

66 Dáil Éireann, 11 May 1937, de Valera's speech on Bunreacht na hÉireann in Maurice Moynihan (ed.), *Speeches and statements by Eamon de Valera* (Dublin, 1980), p. 334. 67 Fanning, *Eamon de Valera*, p. 35. 68 Earl of Longford & Thomas P. O'Neill, *Eamon de Valera: a biography* (Boston, 1971), p. 299. Lee, *Ireland*, p. 211. 69 Ward, *Hanna Sheehy Skeffington*, p. 325.

Conclusion

This study began with the 1916 Proclamation of the Republic and ended with the 1937 constitution. It asked how Irish society moved from the open, inclusive promises of 1916 to the restrictive Catholic covenant of 1937. This then is the story of the making of inequality. It is an overview of the Free State period, not only of individual pieces of legislation, but of the ways in which these legislative acts interacted and interfaced with one another to generate a gender ideology of domesticity that reinforced a patriarchal society.

The story of 1916 and the Proclamation of the Irish Republic was an evolving one, with most of its promises not implemented until after the Free State period. In many ways, the constitution stood in the way of fulfilling those promises – a fact women pointed out time after time, appealing to the Proclamation as a guarantor of their rights. The legacy of the Free State was inequality; the legacy of the constitution was a conservative Catholic state. Both have seeped into modern Ireland. For example, divorce was approved, but only by referendum on 24 November 1995.

The Proclamation, at its core, pledged a sweeping reorganization of Irish society – from ownership of the land to the role of women. It was, at its heart, revolutionary. After the Treaty, however, emphasis quickly shifted from the idea of a revolution affecting all of society to one which focused on political modification, replete with a change of cast, but only substituting one group of male characters for another. It appears as if one apparent goal of the political revolution was to maintain a male political elite to the exclusion of all others. What seemed to be most important in the days of the revolutionary period was independence from England – at the expense of a social revolution.

At the negotiating table to end the Anglo-Irish War, there were multiple positions, raising a plethora of questions. What would the British offer? Was the threat of terrible and immediate war a real one? What was possible and what was acceptable? Was a stepping-stone theory of independence sufficient? Should more emphasis have been given to the republican position? Would it have made any difference if de Valera had been sent to London as part of the negotiating team? Was there any chance that social concerns would have been considered? Would that have been possible?

There is no concensus. I would suggest that the political concerns were too narrow. They limited the Anglo-Irish struggle to a political revolution, while the Proclamation made it more of a social revolution. While the Treaty dealt with vital issues, it is also important to see past the external affairs of the state. Looking beyond the discussions on the Treaty and what it did and did not offer, it is instructive to consider, for example, each group's attitude toward women. In analyzing the respective legislative records of Fianna Fáil and Cumann na nGaedheal, it becomes obvious that they were not that dissimilar. Indeed, they had much in common. Each group curried favour with the Catholic church, and both held to a limited and repressive view of women. See, for example, the legislation each passed on birth control, which both made illegal.

A significant conclusion of this study is that patriarchy has persisted – in both the church and the state. Both Cumann na nGaedheal and Fianna Fáil made it a point to create a patriarchal state in which women had only a domestic identity. It seemed as if there was a consciousness that male privilege had to be protected. Why else would the state limit women's access to the public sphere? Legislation was critical in enacting inequality, in providing the framework that would be a bulwark against equality. Why else would the participation of women in the political sphere cause such consternation? Was it just the result of the trauma of the Civil War or was it something deeper that spoke to the need to protect male privilege?

In the 1920s and 1930s, because of the bargain the Free State made with the clergy, the Catholic church controlled morality, regulated education, hospitals, institutions and the like. This bargain, which allowed the Roman Catholic church unfettered control over all who were in the church's care, resulted in rampant abuse. The architecture of containment was the result.

In any analysis of church/state relations in the Free State period, it is worth pointing out that there was a natural affinity between political leaders and the church. Irish male political leaders were brought up in, and came of age in, a society where submission and deference to religious leaders was inculcated in them from a very early age. With rules and regulations that demonstrated contempt for women, the all-male leaders of the church reinforced their belief in the inferiority of women and their power over women. For example, the Catholic church demanded that women be cleansed after giving birth; married women who had broken no laws, skirted no legislation but simply had given birth were treated as unclean. In my view, that demonstrates contempt for women.

The church's treatment of women who in some way violated their laws or conventions was even more deplorable. Institutionalization was the church/state answer – be it in Magdalene laundries or mother and baby homes. Silence and secrecy were the watchwords in institutions in which horrible abuse occurred and, for the most part, went unchecked. It is a story that has only recently come to light. It was a most regrettable part of the Free State's history.

While the bargain between church and state was an accord that was seen at the time as necessary for the survival of the Free State, it is important to ask where was the opposition to Catholic dominance? How was it expressed? More specifically, how was opposition to the church expressed in villages, in families, in homes throughout Ireland? Where were the women? It is an area that requires more research and analysis.

Another variation on this question needs to be asked about the patriarchal church/state agreement: how did ordinary women fare under the patriarchal rule of church/state over the last hundred years? Women, for example, who were told to stay in their homes by the clergy even if they were being beaten. More research needs to be done on violence against women in all its forms – be it in the home, in the revolutionary period or beyond. There was no divorce. How did these women fare? Married women who were told to keep having sexual relations with their husbands by the clergy, as if it were a husband's unqualified right, despite the fact there were a number of children already in the family. There was no birth control. How did these women fare? Did they stay at home, in the home? Did they know their place? Did the attitudes and actions of this particular patriarchal state reinforce the idea that women did not matter, that they should just stay at home and defer to the men in their family? Was this a part of the Ireland of the 1920s and '30s that has lingered on until today shaping attitudes and influencing perceptions?

Generally recognized for its Catholicity, the '37 constitution also has to be recognized for its patriarchal implications. In fact, it can be argued that Catholicism carries patriarchy within it and that there is a symbiotic relationship between the two. Despite all his talk of reform, the current pope has done very little, if anything, to change the status of women.

Yet despite this, Ireland in 2019 is a very different place than it was in the 1920s and 1930s – an easy, simplistic, obvious observation. Yes, much has changed. But not everything. W.B. Yeats was wrong. All has not changed and certainly not changed utterly.

But change has come. Perhaps the most obvious example is that Irish society is no longer homogeneous, but is multicultural and visibly more diverse. A number of referenda have opened up Irish society, legalizing divorce, gay marriage and abortion. It is a different place. Old attitudes linger, of course, but it is a different place. The recent visit of Pope Francis to Ireland highlighted the tension that now permeates the Catholic church.

The role of women has indeed been altered. Currently, a significant number of women are employed outside the home and are climbing up the corporate ladder. In the public sphere, women can now serve on juries, sit in Dáil Éireann, even hold the position of president of Ireland – as did Mary Robinson and Mary McAleese. There has not yet been a woman taoiseach (the actual wielder of power), but the current taoiseach is the son of immigrant parents, young and openly gay – certainly not in the mould of either W.T. Cosgrave or Eamon de Valera. As he himself said in his comments, while in Washington DC in March of 2019 to celebrate St Patrick's Day: 'I stand here, leader of my country, flawed and human, but judged by my political actions, and not by my sexual orientation, my skin tone, gender or religious beliefs.'[1]

It is a definite change – perhaps one that will open up new possibilities and rupture the mentality that affords women only a domestic identity. Issues still abound, but the public sphere is creaking and slowly opening to women. Currently there are thirty-five women serving in the Dáil, approximately 22 per cent of all deputies. It is only a beginning. Ireland ranks 17th out of the 27 EU states in terms of female representation in the main legislative body. It is a potent reminder of the patriarchy of the public sphere.

Despite women's participation in the Anglo-Irish War, and their active involvement in the Civil War, full citizenship as promised in the 1916 Proclamation was denied them in the Free State. Despite the fact that women participated in the struggle for independence, held at least one government position and were an integral part of the revolutionary

1 Adam Taylor, 'Vice President Pence hosts the Irish prime minister and his gay partner for breakfast', *Washington Post*, 14 Mar. 2018.

movement, they were by 1937 defined as having only a domestic identity. The construction of the ideal Irish woman, the ideology of domesticity, lionized women in the private sphere. It glorified pure and virtuous women – all others were hidden away and castigated as sinners or simply walked away. It was not only that legislation like the Juries Acts gave shape and definition to this belief but rather it was an attitude that lingered, indeed still lingers and permeates the political environment. It is the attitude of patriarchy and Catholicism joined together. See, for example, the experience of Mary McAleese, who was 'barred by the Vatican from participating in a conference on women'. Ironically, the meeting was to mark International Women's Day, with the theme of 'why women matter'.[2] The organizers refused to acquiesce to the dictates of the Vatican and 'decided … to move the conference outside the Vatican' and asked McAleese to be the keynote speaker.

There are some historians – both male and female – who dispute the idea of an ideology of domesticity. One historian claims that it is not 'internally consistent enough to be an ideology'.[3] However, I believe that this text demonstrates that the legislation of Cosgrave and de Valera suggests otherwise, that indeed the net effect of patriarchy was to say that a woman's place was in the home.

Was it that the men in power feared too-sweeping changes? Was political change – political independence – enough for male revolutionaries to cope with? Did these male political leaders fear or sense an unwelcome change in women's status and hence resorted to restrictive legislation? Undoing patriarchy would entail undoing some, if not all, of the privileges conferred on men – as Kevin O'Higgins famously or infamously asked 'Who will cook the dinner?' What began as a full-fledged revolution with the Proclamation fluttering with changes that would entail a lessening of male privilege ended with the thud of the '37 constitution, with its emphasis on codifying Catholicism and enforcing patriarchy as well as its determination to demonstrate Ireland's independence from England.

Once successive governments made a bargain with the Catholic church and officials chose to enact their ideas, women were consigned to

2 Patsy McGarry, 'Mary McAleese barred by Vatican from conference on women', *Irish Times*, 2 Feb. 2018. 3 Clear, *Women of the house*, p. 8. Diarmaid Ferriter, 'Pope's visit will do little for image of Church in Ireland', *Irish Times*, 8 Aug. 2018. In it, the author quotes Mary McAleese.

a second-class status. Working in concert, priests and politicians offered many and varied explanations for denying women free and unfettered citizenship. Overall, it amounted to telling women to know their place. Perhaps it was, to use the words Mary McAleese uttered in another context, 'just dressed up misogyny'.[4]

This study also demonstrated the importance of the fact that some women were radicalized during the revolutionary period. Just as the First World War provided women with opportunities in the public sphere – which they were reluctant to give up after the war – so also did the Anglo-Irish War and Civil War. While only a few women gained entry into the Dáil itself, many others made their presence felt outside it. Women like Jennie Wyse Power and her daughter Nancy, as well as Hanna Sheehy Skeffington and her daughter-in-law, Andrée, kept alive the struggle for complete access to the public sphere. This emancipationist strain was passed down through Andrée Sheehy Skeffington and Hilda Tweedy, leading to the founding of the Irish Housewives Association, through to the modern-day Irish feminist movement. This is a prestigious lineage and will, perhaps, someday lead to the making of full and complete equality.

Bibliography

ARCHIVES AND MANUSCRIPTS

Bureau of Military History
Dublin Diocesan Archives
IWWU Archives
National Archives of Ireland
National Library of Ireland Manuscript Collections
NUWGA Collection
Sheehy Skeffington Collection, NLI
University College, Dublin Archives

NEWSPAPERS

Cork Examiner   *Irish Press*
Dundalk Democrat   *Irish Times*
Irish Catholic   *Kilkenny People*
Irish Independent   *Voice of Labour*

OFFICIAL PUBLICATIONS

Bunreacht na hÉireann.
Mary Immaculate Training College Annual, 1927–9.
Official Reports of the Debates of Dáil Éireann, 1922–37
Official Reports of the Debates of Seanad Éireann, 1922–32
Report of the Committee on Evil Literature
Report of the Committee on the Criminal Law Amendment Act and Juvenile Prostitution

BOOKS AND ARTICLES

Alexander, M. Jacqui, 'Not just (any) body can be a citizen: the politics of law, sexuality and postcoloniality in Trinidad and Tobago and the Bahamas', *Feminist Review*, 48 (1994).
Arensberg, Conrad M., *The Irish countryman: an anthropological study* (Long Grove, IL, 1937).
Beatty, Aidan, *Masculinity and power in Irish nationalism, 1884–1938* (London, 2016).
Bew, Paul, & Henry Patterson, *Sean Lemass and the making of modern Ireland* (Dublin, 1982).
Bock, Gisela & Susan James, *Beyond equality and difference* (London, 1992).

Bourke, Angela et al. (eds), *Field Day anthology of Irish Writing, v: Irish women's writings and traditions* (Cork, 2002).

Broderick, Eugene, *John Hearne* (Dublin, 2017).

Cahill, Edward, *Irish Monthly* (1924–5).

Cahillane, Laura, *Drafting the Irish Free State constitution* (Manchester, 2016).

Caldwell Lesley, 'Reproducers of the nation: women and the family in fascist policy' in David Forgacs (ed.), *Rethinking Italian fascism* (London, 1986).

Clarke, Kathleen, *Revolutionary woman*, ed. Helen Litton (Dublin, 1991).

Clear, Caitríona, *Women of the house: women's household work in Ireland, 1926–1961* (Dublin, 2000).

Clear, Caitríona, 'Women in de Valera's Ireland, 1932–48: a reappraisal' in Gabriel Doherty & Dermot Keogh (eds), *De Valera's Ireland* (Cork, 2003).

Clear, Caitríona, 'Fewer ladies, more women' in John Horne (ed.), *Our war: Ireland and the Great War* (Dublin, 2018).

Colum, Mary, *Life and the dream* (Dublin, 1966).

Conlon, Lil, *Cumann na mBan and the women of Ireland* (Kilkenny, 1969).

Cooney, John, *John Charles McQuaid, ruler of Catholic Ireland* (Dublin, 1999).

Daly, Mary E., 'Women, work and trade unionism' in Margaret MacCurtain & Donnchadh Ó Corráin (eds), *Women in Irish society* (Dublin, 1978).

Daly, Mary E., *Industrial development and Irish national identity, 1922–1939* (Syracuse, 1992).

Daly, Mary E., 'Women in the Irish Free State, 1922–39: the interaction between economics and ideology', *Journal of Women's History*, 6:4 & 7:1 (Winter/Spring, 1995).

Daly, Mary E., *Women and work in Ireland* (Dublin, 1997).

de Grazia, Victoria, *How fascism ruled women: Italy, 1922–1945* (Berkeley, 1992).

de Vere White, Terrence, *Kevin O'Higgins* (Dublin, 1948).

Earner-Byrne, Lindsey, 'Reinforcing the family: the role of gender, morality and sexuality on Irish welfare policy, 1922–44', *History of the Family*, 13:4 (Jan. 2008).

Fanning, Ronan, *Independent Ireland* (Dublin, 1983).

Fanning, Ronan, *Eamon de Valera: a will to power* (London, 2015).

Farrell, Brian, *Sean Lemass* (Dublin, 1993).

Ferriter, Diarmaid, *The transformation of Ireland, 1900–2000* (London, 2004).

Ferriter, Diarmaid, *Judging Dev* (Dublin, 2007).

Ferriter, Diarmaid, *Occasions of sin* (London, 2009).

Foster, R.F., *Modern Ireland, 1600–1972* (London, 1988).

Foster, R.F., *Vivid faces: the revolutionary generation in Ireland, 1890–1923* (London, 2014)

Garvin, Tom, *Judging Lemass* (Dublin, 2009).

Gordon, Linda, 'On difference', *Genders*, 10 (Spring, 1991).

Grazel, Susan R. & Tammy M. Proctor (eds.), *Gender and the Great War* (Oxford, 2017).

Haverty, Anne, *Constance Markievicz: an independent life* (London, 1988).

Horne, John (ed.), *Our war: Ireland and the Great War* (Dublin, 2018).

Jones, Mary, *These obstreperous lassies: a history of the Irish Women Workers' Union* (Dublin, 1988).

Kelly, Bernard, 'Cumann na mBan: a Galway perspective' in Marie Mannion & Jimmy Laffey (eds), *Cumann na mBan: County Galway dimensions* (Galway, 2015).

Kelly, J.M. *The Irish constitution* (Dublin, 1984).

Kennedy, Finola, *Cottage to creche: family change in Ireland* (Dublin, 2001), p. 84.

Keogh, Dermot, 'Church, state and society' in Brian Farrell (ed.), *De Valera's constitution and ours* (Dublin, 1988).

Kerber, Linda, 'Women and the obligations of citizenship' in Linda Kerber, Alice Kessler-Harris & Kathryn Kish Sklar, *US history as women's history: new feminist essays* (Chapel Hill, 1995).

Kiberd, Declan, & P.J. Mathews (eds), *Handbook of the Irish revival* (Dublin, 2015).

Knirck, Jason, *Women of the Dáil: gender, republicanism and the Anglo-Irish Treaty* (Dublin, 2006).

Laffan, Michael, *The resurrection of Ireland* (Cambridge, 1999).

Laffan, Michael, *Judging W.T. Cosgrave* (Dublin, 2014).

Lee, J.J., *Ireland, 1912–1985: politics and society* (Cambridge, 1989).

Longford, earl of & Thomas P. O'Neill, *Eamon de Valera: a biography* (Boston, 1971).

Luddy, Maria, 'Women and politics in Ireland, 1860–1918' in Angela Bourke et al. (eds), *Field Day anthology of Irish Writing, v: Irish women's writings and traditions* (Cork, 2002).

Luddy, Maria, 'Foreword' in Sandra McAvoy et al. (eds), *Sexual politics in modern Ireland* (Dublin, 2015).

MacDonagh, W.P., 'The position of women in modern life', *Irish Monthly* (June 1939).

Mandel, W.F., 'The Gaelic Athletic Association and popular culture, 1884–1924' in Oliver Mac Donagh et al. (eds), *Irish culture and nationalism, 1750–1950* (London, 1983), p. 53.

Marwick, Arthur, *Women at war, 1914–1918* (London, 1977).

Matthew Anne, *Renegades: Irish republican women, 1900–1922* (Cork, 2010).

McCarthy, Cal, *Cumann na mBan and the Irish Revolution* (Cork, 2014).

McCarthy, John P., *Kevin O'Higgins: builder of the Irish state* (Dublin, 2006).

McCoole, Sinéad, *Easter widows*, (Dublin, 2014).

McKillen, Beth, 'Irish feminism and nationalist separatism, 1914–1923', *Éire-Ireland*, 17:4 (1982).

Meehan, Ciara, *The Cosgrave party: a history of Cumann na nGaedheal* (Dublin, 2010).

Mohr, Thomas, 'The rights of women under the constitution of the Irish Free State', *Irish Jurist*, 41 (2006).

Morrison, Eve, 'The Bureau of Military History and female republican activism' in Maryann Valiulis (ed.), *Gender and power in Irish history* (Dublin, 2009).

Moynihan, Maurice, *Speeches and statements by Eamon de Valera* (Dublin, 1980).

Murray, Patrick, *Oracles of God* (Dublin, 2000).

Naughton, Lindie, *Markievicz: a most outrageous rebel* (Newbridge, Co. Kildare, 2016).

Ní Chuilleanáin, Eiléan (ed.), *Irish women: image and achievement* (Dublin, 1985).

O'Connell, T.J., *History of the Irish National Teachers' Organisation* (Dublin, [1970?]).

O'Hegarty, P.S., *The victory of Sinn Féin* (Dublin, 1924).

O'Malley Ernie, *The singing flame* (Dublin, 1978).

O'Neill, Marie, *From Parnell to de Valera: a biography of Jennie Wyse Power* (Dublin, 1991).

O'Riordan, Steven & Sue Leonard, *Whispering hope* (London, 2016).

Owens, Rosemary Cullen, *Louie Bennett* (Cork, 2001).

Pašeta, Senia, *Irish nationalist women, 1900–1918* (Cambridge, 2013).

Pateman, Carole, 'Equality, difference, subordination: the politics of motherhood and women's citizenship' in Gisela Bock & Susan James, *Beyond equality and difference* (London, 1992).

Pateman Carole, *Sexual contract* (Stanford, 1988).

Regan, John M., *The Irish counter-revolution, 1921–1936* (Dublin, 2001).

Richardson, Diane, 'Rethinking sexual citizenship', *Sociology*, 51:2 (2017), 208–24.

Rockett, Kevin, *Irish film censorship* (Dublin, 2004).

Salmon, Marylynn, 'The limits of independence' in Nancy F. Cott (ed.), *No small courage* (Oxford, 2000).

Scott, Joan Wallach, 'Gender: a useful category of historical analysis' in Joan Wallach Scott (ed.), *Gender and the politics of history* (New York, 1988).

Skinnider, Margaret, *Doing my bit for Ireland* (New York, 1917).

Smith, Bonnie, *Ladies of the leisure class* (Princeton, 1981).

Smith, Bonnie, *Changing lives* (Lexington, MA, 1989).

Smith, Harold, *British feminism in the 20th century* (Aldershot, 1990).

Smith, James M., *Ireland's Magdalen laundries* (Notre Dame, 2007).

Staines, Michael, 'The concept of "the family" under the Irish constitution', *Irish Jurist*, (1976).

Steele, Karen, 'When female activists say I' in Gillian McIntosh & Diane Urquart (eds), *Irish women at war* (Dublin, 2010).

Taillon, Ruth, *The women of 1916* (Belfast, 1999).

Tiernan, Sonja, *Eva Gore-Booth* (Manchester, 2012).

Townshend, Charles, *Easter 1916* (London, 2006).

Valiulis, Maryann Gialanella, 'Defining their role in the new state: Irishwomen's protest against the Juries Act of 1927', *Canadian Journal of Irish Studies*, 18:1 (July 1992).

Valiulis, Maryann Gialanella, *Portrait of a revolutionary: General Richard Mulcahy and the founding of the Irish Free State* (Dublin, 1992).

Valiulis, Maryann Gialanella, 'Free women in a free nation: nationalist feminist expectations for independence' in Brian Farrell (ed.), *The creation of the Dáil* (Dublin, 1994).

Valiulis, Maryann Gialanella, 'Gender, power and identity in the Irish Free State', *Journal of Women's History*, 6:4 & 7:1 (Winter/Spring, 1995).

Valiulis, Maryann Gialanella (ed.), *Gender and power in Irish history* (Dublin, 2009).

Ward, Margaret, *Unmanageable revolutionaries* (Dingle, 1983).

Ward, Margaret, 'The League of Women Delegates and Sinn Féin', *History Ireland*, 4:3 (Autumn, 1996).

Ward, Margaret, *Hanna Sheehy Skeffington* (Dublin, 1997).

Weihman, Lisa, 'Doing my bit for Ireland: transgressing gender in the Easter Rising', *Éire-Ireland*, 39:3–4 (Fall/Winter, 2004).

Index